Dear

Thank y
for your help and
patience
Sharad
10·2·2018

The Experimental Cook

A new approach to the art of cooking

Sharad Pradhan

http://www.fast-print.net/bookshop

The Experimental Cook
Copyright © Sharad Pradhan 2018

ISBN: 978-178456-529-9

The right of Sharad Pradhan to be identified as the author of this work has
been asserted by him in accordance with the Copyright, Designs and
Patents Act 1988 and any subsequent amendments thereto.

A catalogue record for this book is available from the British Library

First published 2018 by
FASTPRINT PUBLISHING
Peterborough, England.

IN GRATITUDE

The idea of the book first came to me four years ago while sitting at the bedside of my wife who was hospitalised as a result of a stroke. After overhearing other patients and visitors conversations I thought a book like this would be quite useful to some people.

I have had a lot of help in writing this book especially from my family members who commented on the contents and suggested ideas for the cover design. In particular, I would like to mention my elder sister Shalini who looked through the recipes and suggested various ideas for the cover. I am thankful to my granddaughter Jzuee for her critical comments on the final design of the cover.

I owe gratitude to Claire Ruben of Faire Copy for her comments and contribution. She patiently went through many versions of the manuscript as she had done before with my other two books. Many thanks are due to Theresa Loosley from Print on Demand, the publishers, for helping me with my many queries.

Many thanks are due to my art teacher Jonathan Newey of Jonathan Newey Fine Art Ltd who patiently taught me the very basics of the science and art of watercolour painting. This has been useful to me as an analogy that I have used in this book.

And finally this book would not have been written without the encouragement and help of my dear late wife Nalini who patiently taught me the basics of cooking that I have put into this book

CONTENTS

Dedication   1

Foreword   3

A walk through the book   7

Let's start at the beginning   11

Part I: The science of cooking   **15**

1. Housekeeping and kitchen management   17

2. Storing ingredients and food   21

3. Equipment   25

4. Basic ingredients for you to make a start   33

5. Your laboratory   35

6. Techniques and processes   43

Part II: The art of cooking: practice, variations and creating your own recipes   **59**

7. An easy start   63

8. Disaster recovery   81

9. About morphing   85

10. Making the basic spice mixtures for all curries and vegetables   89

11. Useful hints   113

Part III: Your staple ingredients and how to cook them 123

12. Rice   129

13. Potatoes   139

14. Pasta and noodles   143

15. Couscous   147

16. Breads   149

17. Meat, poultry, fish and shellfish   151

18. Pulses and daals   155

19. Soups   159

20. Vegetables   163

21. Sprouting   167

Part IV: The art of experimenting   169

22. Soups, snacks, dips and raitas   173

23. Vegetables, daals and main meals   201

24. Desserts   257

Part V: References   269

25. The chemistry of cooking   271

26. What can I do with these? Some ideas for your
    experiments   295

27. Where to go from here   305

28. Further reading   307

Index   309

THIS BOOK IS DEDICATED TO

The loving memory of Nalini
My dear wife and companion of 65 years

Who has taught me many of the skills of cooking
And encouraged me to experiment.

FOREWORD

Why this book?

We all need to eat, but not everyone bothers to try their hand at cooking. When forced into a situation of surviving by using their own cooking skills, many resort to some rudimentary basic meals, or takeaways or supermarket ready-made meals.

This is particularly true when older people are left to cook for themselves or for their spouse who has been the main cook in the house before becoming incapacitated. I know this situation very well because I have been through it. The worst case is when your partner has left you, or passed away and you are suddenly left on your own with no one to advise you.

The ability to cook something that one can enjoy and to vary the dishes from day to day, so that one can look forward to the meal rather than be bored with it, is essential in this situation.

What is different about the approach in this book?

The Experimental Cook is a different kind of book. It is NOT a cookery book, NOT an instruction manual nor a book on food technology and science; but a sort of guide to help and encourage you into the art and science of cooking by experimenting with the ideas, techniques and processes explained in this book. The aim is that you will be able to produce interesting and varied foods that you, and also others, can enjoy. We are not talking about gourmet foods, fancy cheffy dishes and complicated recipes; in fact here you will find very few recipes as such, mostly ideas that you can experiment and play with and develop using whatever ingredients you happen to have and the processes that you can easily manage. All you need is to want to start cooking.

This book is not about cooking dishes from a particular cuisine, it is just about understanding how to cook food. There are references to cooking meat and vegetables in Western, Asian and also Chinese style. You will find a lot of information about spices, and cooking curries and vegetables using them. The reason for including this information is that cooking curries and vegetables this way is a better way for experimental cooks to learn because one does not have to use exact proportions of ingredients and there is a lot of room for variations and experimentation. Besides, you can use curries in a similar manner to stews for serving with potatoes, mash, couscous or maybe even chips and you can serve stew with rice. Same with the side vegetables. Just use a little less spice if you want. You could say this is a sort of fusion cooking.

The alternatives

Of course you may say, 'I can rely on takeaways or ready-made foods from the shops.' That may be useful for an occasional change or when you are too busy; but as a long-term solution and value for your money, it is not a practical idea. Ready-made meals and takeaways, besides being expensive and of doubtful nutritional value, could soon become boring. But cooking for yourself, you cook what you want and how you want. The cost would probably be less, the taste better and the nutritional value within your control, depending on which ingredients you choose and how you cook them.

So what would you achieve?

The reason this book is titled *The Experimental Cook* is because it is just that! After learning a few basic techniques (just enough for you to get going), you can start experimenting, learning through your successes and mistakes. There are many separate chapters that will help you along the way.

How to use this book: my suggestions

For an overall idea, please refer to the walk-through page that follows. It is recommended that those new to cooking should read Part I: The Science of Cooking and Part II: The Art of Cooking before attempting to try any cooking. However, for those who are eager to get on with experimenting, I have rearranged the order of titles in the contents page. I recommend that you read them in the order stated below. You can refer to the rest of the book as you go along and progress.

A WALK THROUGH THE BOOK –
A QUICK GUIDE FOR THE READERS

Starter chapters to get you going quicker

The following chapters will help you to make a good start and increase your range of experimenting.

1 Housekeeping and Kitchen Management

Useful hints and tips to look after your workplace and work safely and efficiently. Basic hints to look after your equipment and ingredients.

5 Your Laboratory

Get to know the common ingredients as chemicals.

6 Techniques and Processes

The various processes and techniques used in cooking. You will notice that different processes of cooking and food preparation produce different results. Once acquainted, it will help you to experiment with the right ones.

8 Disaster Recovery

Everyone makes mistakes sometimes. You can recover from some of them. Here are some ideas.

3. Equipment:
Equipment that improves your range of cooking experiments, and saves time.

4 Basic Ingredients for you to Make a Start
The very basic ingredients you may need.

9 About Morphing
How to change some of the ready-cooked, leftover or other food items into something else to make it more interesting to suit your taste. You may want to try these techniques if you are an absolute beginner, to gain confidence.

Chapters that will help you later to improve your skills

10 Making the Basic Spice Mixtures for all Curries and Vegetables
You can make virtually all the curries, vegetables and sauces using techniques and ideas in this section. You can use them for stews, goulash, soups, pies and other dishes too! This section also has a list of all the ingredients you may need and guidance on their use.

11 Useful Hints
Labour- and time-saving hints and tips.

21 Sprouting
This is a very much overlooked area for producing interesting, healthy and tasty additions to salads and other

snacks. You will find techniques and some ideas here; the rest is up to you to experiment more.

Chapters to look through individually as you get along

The information contained in Part III, 'Your Staple Ingredients And How To cook Them' is the core of this book. It will teach you the basics of how to cook various types of food, irrespective of the recipes. This will provide you with the fundamental skills to tackle most of the common food items, to experiment with your own ingredients and processes, and to create your own recipes. I am confident that you will soon be cooking meals that you and others will enjoy.

For your reference at any time

25 The Chemistry of Cooking

This section explains the nature of different chemicals present in our daily foods, and the way they change and react during the various cooking processes. You will find it very useful as a reference to understand the science of cooking and help you in your experimenting with various processes and ingredients.

26 What Can I Do With These?

Sometimes one is left with leftovers like cooked items, vegetables and other odds and ends. Very often these are left to one side till they become unusable and are then thrown away. Actually, even small quantities of leftovers can be put to good use and are excellent for your experimentation. This section will give you some ideas.

And finally: Part IV: The Art Of Experimenting And Some Dishes For You To Try

The recipes contained here are sort of templates which you can vary. There are some simple ideas and suggested variations. You may not find an exact quantity of ingredients here but an approximate idea of the proportions of the various ingredients. This is done deliberately so that you will learn to experiment, and learn how to bring about the taste you like. After all, if you want exact recipes there are plenty of cookery books and online recipes. Following an exact recipe is like painting by numbers. What we are aiming for is a bit of adventurous experimentation. Do not worry; there is always some guidance about sensible proportions of various ingredients, so you will not go far wrong! You can always refer to Section 10 which gives information on most ingredients that you will need and guidance for their use.

LET'S START AT THE BEGINNING

This is probably not the first time you have had a go at cooking? Am I right? I say this because otherwise you probably would not have picked up this book.

You may have done some sort of cooking, or very little, or none at all. You might have tried and got frustrated and resorted to takeaways or junk food. Actually cooking – and we are not talking about gourmet or fancy cooking – is not too difficult to learn and is in fact an enjoyable pursuit. After all, you need to eat and eat well; then why not learn to do it properly? Using some of the techniques in this book you can produce interesting snacks and meals for yourself and for others as well. All you require is an understanding of the basics, some patience and some experimentation.

Like many practical arts, cooking is both a science and an art. A similar example would be watercolouring. You may ask what there is in common between watercolouring and cooking? Let me explain.

Like cooking, watercolouring is both an art and a science. Unless you have a natural gift, you need to know about different types and textures of paper to use, what the paints are made of, the various types of pigment and the way they work. You will also need to know different kinds of brush and how to use various strokes to produce the right effect. You have to understand how to mix different colours and how many are too many. The best way to learn the art of watercolour is by understanding these basic principles and then experimenting.

Cooking is just the same. Of course some persons are natural cooks and they do not need all this preparation. This book contains information on both the science and the art aspect and helps you to have a running start for experimenting.

In my particular case, having never done any sort of painting before, I was very much concerned about the final outcome of my painting during the workshops. My painting did not quite look l like the one I was copying nor like other people's paintings. My teacher put me at ease by saying, "Sharad, your painting is your interpretation of the one you are copying from. It has not got to look like other people's painting. It is fine as long as you like it and are happy with it. Keep practising using the techniques I have shown you and you will get better and better." I will give you the same advice with your cooking experiments.

This analogy between the two arts is quite useful and I will be using it from time to time for emphasising my point. I think you will find it quite helpful.

About the technique of experimental cooking

I would like to explain a bit more how the technique of experimental cooking will help you to break through the barrier of your inability to cook. If you take only one main ingredient, like lamb meat for example, you have many hundreds of different recipes available. This is because they are based on different combinations of other ingredients, spices and cooking techniques. They came about as a result of chefs experimenting with them. Of course you only get to see the successes! Any failures are looked at and improved till they get an acceptable result. In this book you will learn the basic techniques based on the science of cooking (see the reference section), the basic ingredients and their use and some ideas you could experiment with to combine these into some interesting recipes.

PART I: THE SCIENCE OF COOKING

As stated before, cooking is a mixture of science and art. Knowledge of science will help you to appreciate how the different cooking processes work, why you have to follow a certain method for some ingredients and why some of your preparations did not come out as you expected, even though you followed a perfectly good recipe, so that next time you can make the necessary adjustment or correction. Sometimes you may even come up with your own variation; that is experimental cooking for you.

You do not have to follow any recipe exactly. The best way to learn cooking is to use a recipe as a template, but then change the ingredients you have and the processes you can manage. Chefs do this all the time and come up with their new recipes. Use standard recipes of your choice as a template or guide and experiment with them. Do not worry about making mistakes. Even experienced scientists have come up with new knowledge through some of their mistakes while experimenting. Understanding how the processes work will help you a great deal in your experimentation.

You will find some essential scientific explanation behind the various processes throughout this book. The scientific explanation is kept to the essential minimum. However, for those who want to know more, there is a section on the chemistry of cooking in the reference section.

1

HOUSEKEEPING AND KITCHEN MANAGEMENT

You can make cooking an enjoyable experience by practising good housekeeping and planning your activities and menus well in advance. Once you start practising and see the benefits, it will become a habit.

Your workplace

General

Your kitchen is a **workplace**. Like any other place of work you need to organise it so that you can work safely and efficiently and also enjoy yourself while working. After all, you have a limited time at your disposal, you need the rest of your time for other activities such as your hobbies or looking after your spouse etc. Here are a few simple rules which might appear to be obvious but are often overlooked.

Safety first: many of the accidents in the home take place in the kitchen. Keeping your kitchen clean and tidy and knowing where everything is helps to make your kitchen a safe environment to work. Do not leave sharp tools like knives or peelers lying about the work top; clean and put them away **every time** you use them. If you spill any liquid or water on the floor wipe it up and ensure the floor is not slippery. A slippery floor is one of the most common cause of falls in the kitchen, especially among the elderly. It is a good idea to have a packet of plasters nearby in case you cut yourself.

Organise the basic dry ingredients such as spices neatly and label them so that you can get at them quickly. Put them back in their place after each use.

Make sure you know what you have stored in your fridge/ freezer; check regularly if any items are going off and discard them. Clean out the interior from time to time.

While cooking

Most of the 'mess' starts when you are cooking. Pots and pans accumulate on the worktop, the sink gets overloaded with unwashed items because the draining board still has many things that have not been dried and put away. A familiar picture? You are not alone! I have gone through this. One of the best pieces of advice my wife has given me is to tidy up and keep the area around the hob clear after each process. Put that chopping board away even though you may want to use it later in the next process. Clean the knife and put it in its place. Clear the backlog of the sink and the draining board. If you keep doing it there will not be so many items to deal with. Then, when you finish cooking and take your food to the table, you will not have so many items to clean when you finish your meal!

Planning

Good planning will help you to work efficiently. Plan your menus for a few days at a time, preferably at the beginning of each week. That way you can match your workload to the other activities you have, such as hospital appointments, recreational activities, meetings etc. You can cook something ahead of a busy day or have an idea to rustle up something quickly from a few ingredients and use the stir-frying or morphing ideas explained in a later part of the book.

I like to use a small white board that has a magnetic surface with the days of the week printed on it. I have it stuck on the fridge with my main activities, the menu for the day and what I need to take out from the freezer for the next day written on it, and I update it each week.

You can do many 'part processes' in advance, even a day before your busy day, such as marinating meat or fish or even chopping onion, as we shall see later in the book. Once you get into the habit of thinking ahead you will not be caught out not having any idea of what to cook. One advantage of being an **experimental cook** is you will soon be able to deal with those 'last minute crises' of having to change your menu or running out of a particular ingredient at the last minute!

Distractions

Imagine this scenario:

You have put something under the grill which needs only about two or three minutes to brown. The telephone rings or there is someone at the door, a neighbour perhaps. You leave your workplace and forget all about the grill until a burning smell attracts your attention back to the kitchen!

One of the best ways to deal with telephone calls is of course have your handset with you or to use an answerphone. However the best overall remedy is always to use a kitchen timer with a loud bell to remind you to come back to attend to whatever process you need to attend in the kitchen.

Cleaning

Keep all the used equipment clean for use the next time. Some frying pans, especially woks that have the surface coated using the 'patina' method when you use them for the first time, only need wiping clean with a tissue. Any used oil should not be poured into the sink, because this will eventually block your outside drains. Instead, clean the pan with a tissue to absorb all the oil and bin the tissue. Wipe the surface of the pan clean before using washing up liquid.

2

STORING INGREDIENTS AND FOOD

Spices

Spices are expensive. You do not need to store them in large quantities. Best is to buy them in smaller lots, but not the small packets (as sold in some supermarkets). Keep them in sealed bags or jars outside near your working area or in the store cupboard. They will last for months, even longer. Eventually, though they do not go bad as such, some spices, especially those containing aromatic oils, will lose their intensity and flavour. For liquid spices, once opened follow the supplier's instructions.

Flours

Reseal any opened unused flour packet and put it in a plastic bag to protect it from being pierced and from moisture. Any clumps in the flour are an indication that moisture has got to it. Taste any old flours before using; an unpleasant or bitter taste indicates it has gone off and should not be used.

Vegetables

Potatoes and onions are best kept in dark, light-proof bags to prevent sprouting. You can buy special bags, which I found work very well and are worth the money. I keep all other fresh vegetables in the fridge, preferably in the vegetable drawer. It is best to remove the packaging as it can accumulate moisture inside and the produce will begin to rot.

Coriander: I must make a special mention of coriander. It is quite expensive and normally you use only a little at a time. Many people complain that it does not last long in the fridge. I can tell you how I do it. Fresh coriander sold in most shops is quite damp from the cleaning process, or if it is not cleaned you will find the roots have soil sticking to them. Either way this is a good start for the rotting process, which does not take too long in the case of coriander. I have had years of experimentation on the best way to keep coriander in good order.

Once home, clean any soil or sand on the roots by dry brushing, but **avoid bruising** the stalks. Take out any leaves that are turning brown or sticky or black – they are the culprits! **Avoid any contact with water.** Wrap it in two layers of newspaper. If you have a large bunch then divide it and make two or more packages, then pack these packages in a plastic box lined with newspaper. Cover them with one more thin layer of newspaper making sure the lid of the box fits tightly. Now wrap another layer of newspaper around the box and put this box in a polythene bag and leave it in the fridge; **not in the vegetable drawer.** Your coriander will last for two to four weeks provided you take it out every four or five days and check the condition of the coriander and the wrappings. If the paper is soggy, change it. Check for any leaves turning brown or black. If the coriander seems to be wet leave it out to dry on a tray before repacking.

Yogurts and creams
Once opened cover the pot in cling film and try to finish by the 'use by' date. I find that the yogurt in the plastic pots

lasts a lot longer if the top of the pot is covered in cling film and the pot stored upside down in the fridge.

Cooked foods

You have spent considerable time and effort in preparing the food. It is a shame to let it go to waste by not storing it properly. Besides, it will save time some other day by not having to cook a full meal. (See leftovers and morphing section).

Store your leftovers in the fridge and use them as soon as possible. See Section 9, About Morphing for creative ideas. You can freeze most of your cooked food such as sauces, curries, stews, and parts of soups (take the watery part out, use it as a clear soup), vegetables, parathas, breads.

Onion: **A useful trick!**

Quite often the size of an onion is larger than you need. I peel the whole onion, slice part of it for use in my recipe and put the rest (uncut) in a small plastic box with a tight lid. It lasts for a couple of days after which it starts becoming a bit waterlogged. This method is also useful if you have too much to do the next day (like cooking for guests etc.). In this case I peel and halve the quantity of onions the day before; it also saves mess around the worktop.

KITCHEN MANAGEMENT AND
STORING SUMMARY

1	Organise your workplace.
2	Safety first: look after sharp tools, wipe up any spills on the floor.
3	Organise and label dry ingredients.
4	Check the contents of the fridge/freezer regularly and keep it clean.
5	Plan your activities and menus ahead and update regularly.
6	Keep the area around the hob clear at all times.
7	Clear the sink and draining board area after each process to avoid backlog of items awaiting cleaning.
8	Avoid burning or overcooking due to distractions, use a timer to remind you.
9	Take care of your dry ingredients such as spices and flours.
10	Keep onions and potatoes in dark bags.
11	Look after fresh vegetables, especially delicate leaf ones like coriander, using the technique described here.
12	Freeze your leftovers.

3

EQUIPMENT

You have probably already got most of the basic equipment listed here, which you will need for your experimental cooking. There is no reason not to proceed with your experiments even if you do not have some of the items; you can get them as you go along. However there are some items essential for a good start, as you will see from my comments. I have not listed items such as a microwave cooker or toaster because everyone has them nowadays.

Utensils

I believe that you will be normally cooking just for yourself or one another person. Therefore you will need smaller pots and saucepans with lids, frying pans (small and large) and a small one-egg frying pan. I find the small 5 inch (about 12.5 cm) one-egg frying pan that I have very useful. I can fry just one egg or shallow fry small fishcakes with very little oil, and it is also very useful for seasoning with spices in hot oil for various oriental dishes that I will mention later in the book.

Wok

A good wok is absolutely essential. Get one about 8 to 10 inches in diameter that you can handle easily. Mine is 8 inches in diameter and I find it quite adequate. The very large ones are difficult to handle and waste oil. With the wok you can cook several dishes without having to use different pans. Another useful trick you can perform with the wok is that you can, for example, fry onion and push it to the side of the wok and, in the same juices or oil, add meat for browning. When this is done you can mix the two and carry on with the next process of adding items and cooking. This is where the planning and organising comes, as we shall see in the processes.

You will need microwave-proof dishes and bowls for use with the microwave, and oven-proof dishes and trays for use with the oven or grill.

Cutting and scraping tools

Good knives are absolutely essential, not only for efficient slicing and chopping but for safe working. Get a largish knife that you can handle easily. I see people using a small 5 or 6 inch knife for slicing or chopping. It is inefficient and you are more likely to cut your fingers in the process. A good all-purpose knife should be at least 8 inches (20 cm) long with about 1.5 inches (3.5 cm) width near the handle end and pointed at the other end. When you pick it up you should feel it is well balanced and with a good grip. We will talk more about using the knife during the processes part of the book.

You will need one or two other smaller knives for paring and peeling, and for cleaning shellfish such as prawns.

Knives are only good if they are kept sharp. A good knife sharpener is essential. I like the one that has four sharpening slots. Two for each side of the blade, each side has a rough and a fine slot.

A peeler, preferably with a swivelling blade, is a better option than some rigid blade ones. I would recommend two graters. A cheap pyramid-shaped one with different grating shapes and the other a more expensive fine micro-plane grater. The micro-plane grater is really worth the money because you can grate cheese and similar things very finely to garnish soups and pastas, to add to the fillings of wraps or as toppings for cheese on toast, and it has endless other uses.

Scissors are very handy as an alternative means of cutting leaf vegetables, coriander and vegetable stems. You will need finely pointed sharp kitchen scissors for this. I would also recommend that you have another sharp and robust meat scissor for cutting through joints and slicing or trimming meat like bacon or ham etc.

Chopping board

The chopping board should have two good surfaces. Use one for vegetables etc. and the other for meats. That way you can avoid contamination from raw meats to other items. There are also plastic mats available so that you can use different ones for meats and vegetables.

Measuring and timing

Experienced cooks often judge the amount of various ingredients; as an experimenter you need to measure or weigh the main items. It is good practice anyway. Normally there is no need to measure exactly small ingredients such as spices, but there are a few spices such as chilli, turmeric and asafoetida that need to be used with caution so as not to spoil the taste. We will come to that in the processes and recipe sections.

For volumetric measuring a jug with markings for pints, millilitres and ounces is very useful. For small measures, get a set of measuring spoons. Kitchen scales are essential. I like the digital ones. I have small portable electronic ones about 17 cm square with a choice of units in grams, kg, pounds, ounces etc. You can use any container and zero-in its weight before adding the items.

A simple countdown mechanical timer with a loud bell is very useful, as mentioned in the kitchen management section.

Sieves and colanders

A metal or plastic sieve for flour, and a large colander for draining foods from cold and hot water (like washed vegetables or pasta) is very useful. Get a colander that has two handles for easy lifting.

Spoons and ladles

A couple of large-size serving spoons and ladles to take out liquid from pans is recommended. A slotted spoon to lift food out of liquid or oil is very useful.

Skewers

One or two barbecue-type skewers for prodding and testing meats and cakes etc.

Grinders and pestle and mortar

I like small grinders that can grind dry ingredients and can be used for making wet paste and chutneys as well. A hand-held or free-standing liquidiser can be useful for soups; you can get one later as needed. A small pestle and mortar is useful to pound spices.

Speciality equipment

I would recommend the following items that will enhance your range of experimentation, make your cooking easy and also produce delicious food.

Slow cooker

I use mine regularly for making soups, curries and stews. Soups are quite easy to make with a slow cooker using fresh meats, vegetables, leftovers, pulses etc. as we will see later in the book.

Steamer

You can do without it by using a saucepan and a plate with holes like a sieve but best is to get a simple electric steamer. They consist of a stack of plastic containers with a lid, sitting on a lower container with water. There is an electric timer (up to about 25 minutes or so). The generated steam passes through holes in the bottom of the containers producing steamed vegetables without them getting waterlogged and soggy. You can have delicious steamed vegetables like carrots, peas, sweetcorn, spinach, celery etc.

Wraps, films and paper

Aluminium foil is useful for cooking as well as storing. Cling film is something I cannot do without. Greaseproof paper is very useful for lining baking trays.

The items listed in this section are the very basic and most probably you already have something similar. Start with what you have and add on as you need according to your experience.

EQUIPMENT SUMMARY

I recommend that you should have the following equipment from the very start, apart from the pots and pans, oven, hob and microwave that every kitchen will have.

1   A good sharp knife and knife sharpener and a chopping board.

2   Kitchen scissors for use instead of knife when convenient.

3   Volumetric measuring for liquids: a pint jug, and spoons (tablespoon, teaspoon etc.)

4   A good kitchen scale.

5   An electric grinder or pestle and mortar.

6   A colander and a large slotted spoon.

7   Frying pan and a wok.

8   A simple kitchen winding countdown timer up to one hour.

4

BASIC INGREDIENTS FOR YOU TO MAKE A START

There are many ingredients that you may be using. It is not intended to list all of them here as you will find them in many recipes, for example many types of vegetables (fresh and canned), fruit, meats and processed meats like sausages and bacon, different types of flours etc.

The ingredients listed here are the most useful ones for experimental cooks to try their hand at cooking.

Potatoes

Various kinds of rice

Flours: Wholemeal, plain, self-raising, rice flour etc.

Pasta and noodles: especially rice noodles, egg noodles, spaghetti and macaroni

Couscous: especially pre-cooked

Cooked prawns

Sausages

Canned vegetables and beans: especially sweetcorn, beans, baked beans

Soups: in packets and canned

Salad material: lettuce, spring onions, carrots and tomatoes

Bakery items: breads, wholemeal rolls, crumpets

Sauces: such as dark soya sauce, chilli sauce, Lea and Perrins sauce, tomato ketchup, etc.

Fresh seasoning, spices and herbs: Ginger, garlic, coriander, thyme, marjoram, bay leaves, basil, etc.

Spices, whole: cumin, coriander, nutmeg, cloves, cinnamon bark, green cardamoms, black pepper, whole dried red chilli, black mustard seeds, fenugreek seeds

Spices, powdered: cumin, coriander, turmeric, clove and cinnamon mixture, chilli, cayenne pepper

Oils and butters: vegetable or sunflower oil, extra virgin olive oil, ghee, butter, margarine

Dairy products: milk, yogurt

Other: salt (rock and table), sugars (granulated white, brown etc.), mustard paste, baking soda, citric acid, tartaric acid, tomato paste, etc.

SUMMARY

1   Most of the commonly used ingredients are listed above. If you do not have a particular item, you can try to substitute something similar.

2   More information about some of the ingredients, where necessary, will be found in the processes, recipes and reference sections.

3   Regarding Asian spices: Supermarket packs are small and relatively expensive. Try buying from ethnic shops in larger and cheaper packs if you use a lot of them. They do keep a fairly long time if kept in airtight jars. You can buy whole spices and grind them to powder as required.

5

YOUR LABORATORY

Look around your kitchen. You have probably more different chemicals than an average laboratory. These chemicals are in all sorts of ingredients in your store cupboard, your vegetable rack, your fridge and freezer. I will mention a few of them in a moment.

So, you have bought a nice ham sandwich for lunch. You can look at it as your lunch but it is also a cocktail of different chemicals such as sugar, carbohydrate, starch, fat, enzymes, minerals and vitamins.

When you are cooking or creating new recipes you are processing or experimenting with different chemicals and their reactions with each other. The cooking process is probably more complex than the laboratory experiments that scientists do. They have a few chemicals at a time and use controlled methods to experiment with them. You are playing with many chemicals and probably have much less control, but the good thing is that whatever the outcome of your experimentation you are probably producing something that you can enjoy eating and also, if you keep your scientific hat on, you can learn a lot and improve your cooking. **That is the basis of being an experimental cook.**

If you have a little understanding of these food chemicals and their behaviour you can manipulate lots of processes and take advantage of their reactions. For example you will know the answers to questions such as: why do certain things dissolve? What is an emulsion? What is the secret of making a good sauce? Why does the gravy become lumpy? Why does overcooked meat become inedible? Why does food stick to the pan? What are the differences between oils and fats? And many more. We will deal with this information in the processes section.

Have you wondered why there are different methods, temperatures and timings for cooking various meats? Why some meats are quickly pan fried, some deep fried and some cooked for a long time in the oven? This is to do with the behaviour of various chemicals in the food during the cooking processes. We will deal with this in the reference section.

For now we are keeping the information overload to the minimum as our main aim is to make you aware of the scientific facts but, more importantly, to start experimenting.

It is important for all of us to understand what happens to the various ingredients during the process of cooking. You may have a basic knowledge of chemistry but may not be aware of the application of this knowledge to the cooking of foods.

Let us look at what chemicals are lurking in your kitchen.

Proteins

These are found in all types of meats and fish, milk and dairy products. These are special molecules that are sensitive to food chemicals, enzymes, heat and water and change their appearance and behaviour during various cooking processes. Some types of proteins will stretch and form long strings while others may join together to form a sticky, complex three-dimensional network. This process is called denaturing, that is, changing the natural state.

There are many types of proteins associated with a variety of chemicals called amino acids. However, for our purpose there are two basic types. One we would call water lovers and the other water haters. These affect the behaviour of many substances during the various cooking processes such as making sauces, cooking vegetables, meats etc. We will come to that later in the book. For now it is important to note that knowing a little about these chemicals will help you to understand why some foods are better cooked using a certain method and why some processes do not work properly. In short it will help you to be an experimental cook and try a variety of processes.

Yogurt and cheeses are a good example of how the proteins change. The friendly bacteria used make them unfold the proteins in the milk, which becomes thicker and gel-like and changes to yogurt. By further processing the gel-like yogurt we get a solidified version in the form of cheese.

Carbohydrates

These are the molecules used by plants to store energy in the form of sugars and starches, and the fibre which the plants use to build their walls and cells: a sort of structural material. The fibre contains cellulose, gum and pectin. When we cook plant-based ingredients we are changing the structure of these molecules. The fibre including pectin does not contribute to nutrition but has important dietary functions such as slowing down absorption of glucose. The appearance, taste and flavour of the vegetables change depending on how the carbohydrates are affected by various cooking processes, temperatures and other ingredients used while cooking.

Starches

These are carbohydrates and the main chemicals in grain flours like wheat, corn and barley, and are also found in plants like potatoes. Starches are usually associated with proteins. Starches from different sources have different properties, for example the starch from corn flour or the starch from plain flour, as we will see later when we look at the processes. Essentially they consist of long threaded molecules wound tightly like a ball and packed densely in granules. When the granules are cooked in a liquid they swell by absorbing some of the liquid thus creating a thick body, such as you see in sauces, or a sticky mass such as you see in gravies, or a solid structure when baked, as seen in breads.

Sugars

Sugars are basically chemically classified as sucrose. They are obtained from plants such as sugar cane, sugar beet, and palm and also from insects such as bees. All plants store their energy in the form of sugar; that is why we find many fruits and berries so sweet. The most commonly used sugar is the 'table sugar'. There are various other types of sugars available such as brown sugar, icing sugar, caster sugar etc. We also use sugar in the form of honey, sugar syrup and molasses. Another popular type of sugar mainly used in Asian cuisine is jaggery, an unrefined brown sugar made from sugar cane or palm.

Oils and fats

Oils are obtained from various seeds, some grains such as corn, nuts like peanuts and fruit like olives. Fats are animal products, such as butter obtained from dairy foods, and also those obtained directly from animals, like lard. Some fish meat contains oil. Many oily fish, like salmon, sardine, herring, and mackerel, are high in long-chain omega 3 fatty acids which are good for the health. Shark and cod liver oils are well known.

Plants store some of their energy in oil and animals store theirs in fat. Oils have a low melting point and stay in liquid form at normal room temperatures and solidify only when they are chilled, while fats have a higher melting point and solidify at room temperature. They all have different boiling points and therefore require different amounts of heat energy before they start boiling or smoking. This property is used in cooking for different frying techniques.

Oils and fats are basically similar chemical substances and are technically classified as fats. They are further classified as saturated, unsaturated, hydrogenated, omega fats etc. We will not go into the details of the classification as it is not essential for us to get experimenting. The only fact worthwhile knowing is that the fats that are solid at room temperature are saturated fats because of their dense structure and those which are liquid at room temperature are generally in the unsaturated category. One further useful fact to know is that the saturated fats are more resistant to staling and keep for a much longer time than the unsaturated ones. This is why leftover oil may smell a bit off and butter lasts longer without getting rancid.

Vinegars and acids

Vinegars contain acetic acid and are made from fermenting wine, cider etc. They have different strengths of acidity, the standard being the malt vinegar. Stronger vinegars with more complex flavours are produced by distillation and ageing processes. Balsamic vinegar is one of the more expensive vinegars with a strong and distinct aroma, and is used in salad dressings. Vinegars are also useful for pickling.

Lemon and lime juice are the most commonly used acids to provide acidity and flavour to food.

Citric acid and tartaric acid powders are commonly used in baking. They react with bicarbonate of soda and produce carbon-dioxide gas which makes cakes spongy and light.

Tamarind, which is a pulp from a tropical tree pod, is another product that is used extensively in Asian cooking for flavouring. It has some interesting properties that make some vegetables, for example okra, less sticky when cooking.

Salts

Table salt is processed sea or rock salt and is fortified with potassium iodide. Common salt is harvested from the sea. Rock salt is a mineral harvested from salt mines.

Enzymes

We use enzymes indirectly when we use ingredients such as tamarind, amachur (powder from dried green mangoes), sumac (powdered red fruit of the Sumac bush) etc. These change the behaviour of the ingredients and also add flavour and can change the texture of the food being cooked.

Pectin

This is a naturally occurring thickening agent present in the cell walls of plants. During the ripening process pectin is broken down by natural enzymes and the fruit becomes softer. We consume pectin along with our food but it does not contribute to our nutrition. However, you might be interested to know that in the human gut pectin slows down the absorption of glucose by trapping carbohydrates.

Spices and herbs

These contain very strong and aromatic chemicals. Some spices, such as cloves, cinnamon and pepper, contain aromatic oil that is released when roasted or crushed. Herbs can be used in the dried form or you can have fresh herbs. Herbs and spices are used in many pharmaceutical products. The effect of spices and herbs can be overpowering if used in excessive quantity. Using too many different spices in one recipe does not create a flavoursome dish. It is like mixing too many colours together which, as you know, results in a muddy colour.

SUMMARY	
1.	Consider your kitchen as a laboratory full of various chemicals which react in various ways when the food cooks. You will be a better cook if you have the basic information about these reactions, and be able to experiment with your recipes. For detailed information about these ingredients refer to the reference section at the end.
2.	Proteins
3.	Carbohydrates
4.	Starches
5.	Oils and fats
6.	Sugars
7.	Vinegars and acids
8.	Salts
9.	Enzymes
10.	Pectin
11.	Spices and herbs

6

TECHNIQUES AND PROCESSES

Now that we have looked at the ingredients as 'chemicals' in your laboratory, we shall have a look at the processes and techniques you can employ to do your 'experimentation' and use various recipes or create your own.

Techniques

Techniques are the ways you can achieve your objective in an efficient and more effective way. For example making a smooth sauce without lumps, cooking vegetables that taste and look nice and green, and creating the right texture and appearance like crispy or smooth, slicing and cutting vegetables and onions safely etc.

Processes

When it comes to cooking, the word 'process' does not comes into our minds. However we all know that food can be cooked in various ways and using different methods; each has a different effect on the texture, taste and appearance of the final product.

The processes are basically the sequence and methods used to change the various ingredients into the dish you are making. Most of the processes require application of heat in some way such as boiling, frying, grilling, steaming, baking, microwaving etc. However certain processes do not involve heat, for example marinating, soaking, freezing etc. We will look at some of these processes in this part the book.

The processes and science go hand in hand. The information about science will help you use the various processes more effectively and understand why some of the results turned out differently than you expected, and practising the right techniques will help to you to achieve your objectives. There is a reference section on the science of cooking at the end of the book. I will explain the essential facts as required during various processes.

My approach to techniques and processes

I use the word 'techniques' as just the way we use the methods that are supplementary to the processes. I will not be dealing with them separately, they will pop up as hints throughout the book.

There are several little techniques that we will come across during various processes. I shall mention them in their appropriate context during the recipe section and in some cases in the reference section on the science of cooking. However there is one thing every cook needs to do and that is to slice, cut or chop vegetables.

Chopping, cutting, slicing food

We see chefs slicing or chopping food like some sort of machine. Rather than imitate them I would advise you to pay more attention to the knife you are selecting. Make sure you are comfortable with the knife in terms of its length and balance and ensure that it is sharp. A good chopping knife has a profile (slightly curved). You use different parts of the profile for slicing and chopping. Best is to observe how a chef uses the knife for slicing and chopping. The shape and size of the cut (onions for example) has an effect on how the vegetables cook and how they mix with the rest of the ingredients of the dish. I am stressing this point because it is often overlooked. You will find that the recipes often call for the food to be 'sliced', 'chopped', 'into batons', 'into small cubes' etc. You should pay attention to it.

A well balanced knife with a blade about 8 inches long is best suited for the job. Some people use a very short knife which in fact makes the job more difficult and unsafe. Slicing vegetables requires a horizontal movement of the knife while chopping requires a rocking movement using the point of the long knife as a fulcrum and the knife as a lever moving up and down. You need to protect your fingers by keeping them curled up and only your knuckles facing the blade. You can further increase safety by holding the blade at a slight angle away from the fingers. It is **not** necessary to perform this task with the speed of TV chefs. You do it at the speed you can manage comfortably and **safely.**

Chopping onion: Many savoury recipes call for sliced or chopped onion. It is important to know how to cut, slice or chop onion. The best way to peel the onion is first to remove any loose skin and then cut it into half. That way you can have edges of the skin to pull off. Another technique is to hold the whole onion under either warm or cold water. Since the outer and inner layers have a different rate of expansion and contraction with heating or cooling the layers separate and are easy to peel.

Finely chopped onion mixes with the food and is good for creating sauce: the finer the better. Too much onion will make the sauce slightly sweeter so if you want hot curry avoid using a large amount of finely chopped onion. You can add roughly chopped or sliced onion instead. Finely sliced onion is good for caramelising which produces a smoky flavour and is often used as a garnish on top of rice dishes such as biryani.

The processes

Cooking processes (including pre- and post-cooking)

There are many ways foods can be cooked in the kitchen, and outdoors as in barbecue and even in a much more primitive way by burying in hot sand. We will consider only some relevant ways that we can easily employ for our purpose. Most of the cooking processes involve application of heat. When direct heat is applied such as cooking in a pan or baking or grilling, controlling the heat is important. It should be remembered that the food keeps on cooking even if the heat is turned off. This also applies to microwaves.

Marinating

Marinating is immersing or soaking meats or fish in some sort of acid-based solution called a marinade. The acids denature (that is change the natural behaviour of) the outer layers of the proteins with which they are in contact, making the layer softer and allowing the marinade to penetrate a little inside the meat or fish. This changes the texture as well the flavour of the items soaking in it.

This is a very useful way of injecting flavour into the food you wish to cook and of great use for all meats and fish dishes. You can make a marinade out of many things for example, different oils, wines, vinegars, lemon juice, honey, chilli sauce, soya sauce, tomato juice, yogurt, spices; the list is endless. You need to get the right combination of the various ingredients you are using. Best is to mix various items first in a small dish; taste as you go along to check if you like it before adding/rubbing into the food to be marinated. Remember that when using spices or items such as 'Garam masala' or Indian spices, the actual taste of the cooked food will be different from the taste of the marinade, which will be quite strong. Lemon juice has a tendency to tenderize and start its own cooking process so, unless you want this, it is better to add lemon juice during the cooking or later after the food is cooked.

Dressings

Interestingly, dressings can have very similar ingredients, like vinegars, yogurt, lemon juice, honey etc. but it is not a cooking process. Dressings are finishing processes such as used on salads to make them more flavoursome.

Marinades and dressings are simple and interesting areas for experimental cooks to investigate and experiment on. **You can learn a lot about which ingredients go together and how flavours change.**

Vinaigrettes

These are versatile type of dressings for salads, made by mixing oils and vinegars (usually those flavoured with various herbs). Crushed mustard is added and the mixture is blended till it emulsifies. They are often used with some Italian dishes. Experimental cooks should try these simple flavourings when making salads.

Boiling and steaming

Water boils at a specific temperature depending upon the atmospheric pressure surrounding it. Pure water boils at 100°C at sea level and at a lesser temperature at higher altitude. Water can transfer heat to the substance immersed in it faster than steam, oil or air. The amount of heat transferred depends upon the temperature of the water. The highest transfer rate is when the water is boiling. A pressure cooker increases the temperature at which the water boils and turns to steam, which contains a lot more heat.

Steaming without additional pressure is useful to cook food without getting it soggy and ensuring it retains its flavour, colour and texture. The Chinese use a woven basket to tenderly cook fish, chicken and vegetables. You can instead use a metal colander to do the same. I have an inexpensive plastic electric steamer consisting of a bottom heating tank with a heating element, a simple countdown timer and two upper compartments. I use it to steam vegetables like carrots, corn and celery which makes a healthy and tasty vegetable side dish in just a few minutes.

Parboiling

This is partly cooking the food near the boiling point for a short time prior to further cooking by another process. As an example, potatoes are often parboiled before baking in the oven with other food such as meat or chicken.

Simmering and braising

These are methods of cooking food at a temperature below the boiling temperature of the liquid used. Continuing to cook the food in the same liquid without boiling is called simmering. These processes are usually used when cooking more delicate foods or to retain certain flavours and textures. Simmering with the lid on is used to cook food without much loss of liquid due to evaporation. It involves controlled heat and is often used in nearly cooked food with a lot of sauce, like curries and stews, to reduce the liquid content without overcooking the food, in which case the lid is left off.

Braising is a combination method of cooking that uses both dry and moist heat. The food is first seared at a high temperature in a pan or under the grill and then finished off at a lower temperature sitting in some sort of liquid in a covered pot. Braising is commonly used to pot-roast meats.

Grilling

Grilling employs a high temperature to cook food and usually requires the food to be turned over half way through the cooking to cook both sides properly. The grills you are most likely to be using would be electric grills or barbecues.

Deep frying and shallow frying

Deep-frying involves immersing the food completely in oil (usually groundnut, sunflower or rapeseed). It produces a crisp outer layer and a softer inside. You can use a deep frying pan or a wok or a purpose-made electric fryer for the job. Shallow frying is a method of cooking in a frying pan with just enough oil to cover food halfway from the bottom and turning over to cook the other side. Shallow frying is less messy, healthy and economical and I prefer to use this method whenever I can. You can get chips that can be cooked in the oven instead of deep-frying them. However there are certain foods that can be properly cooked only by deep-frying.

Stir-frying

Stir-frying is a very useful process especially for the experimental cook. It is mainly used in Chinese-style cooking but you can also use it to create your own dishes. It is a very easy and quick way to cook delicious food. The food is usually thinly diced or cut into small pieces for quick cooking. A very small amount of oil is added to a very hot wok. The food to be cooked is added just as the oil starts smoking. The cooking process involves constantly stirring the food or shaking the wok to distribute the heat evenly through food which cooks in just a few minutes. With stir-frying you can turn even the most uninteresting vegetables into delicious dishes. You will find some ideas in the recipe section.

Baking

Foods such as breads, some puddings and cakes etc. require the baking process. Baking ovens raise the temperature of the air inside the oven that heats the food by radiation bouncing back from the oven walls. Some ovens have electric elements and some employ gas to produce the heat. The ovens can be either convection type or with a fan. Because of the method by which heat is conducted, the baking process takes a longer time to cook food. In order to get the right results it is important to **preheat** the oven to the given temperature and to place the food in the right position in the oven. Sometimes the recipe calls for two different temperatures during the process. This allows the food to rise at a slower rate or cook more thoroughly before browning at the top such as bread. Some bread recipes call for a tray of cold water to be placed on the lower shelf during the earlier part of the baking. This is because in the first minutes the yeast in the dough makes the bread rise rapidly. The rise will be less if a hard crust is formed during this stage. The steam produced helps to keep the bread moist. The tray is normally removed after a few minutes. You can use a skewer to check if the bread is cooked thoroughly. It should be clean when withdrawn without soft sticky dough sticking to it. Some recipes such as cakes call for not opening the oven door and losing the heat before it is cooked which would result in the cake collapsing.

Perhaps this is the right place to explain the difference between the bread making and cake making processes.

To make bread we need glutinous flour, yeast and water. The

water makes sticky sheets of gluten that allows the yeast to multiply. The yeast while baking produces carbon dioxide gas that makes the bread rise. A little salt that is added to the flour slows down the rise so that it continues throughout the baking.

For cakes we do not need glutinous flour. The addition of fats such as butter or oil breaks the strands of any glutinous sheets into smaller strands, hence it is called the shortening process. The result is soft and tender cakes.

Slow cooking

This is my favourite method for cooking delicious soups, stews and for lamb and pork curries. The food is cooked for several hours on a very low heat that brings out natural flavours without having to add too many spices. There is no danger of the food burning because the steam produced recirculates in the cooker. I usually brown the meat or season and sauté the vegetables in a pan before transferring to my electric slow cooker and add any water or stock to it as required. Since the process takes several hours (four to five on average) you can add more tender items during the later part so that they keep their texture. You can taste the preparation as it cooks and adjust the flavour to your taste by adding any spices, herbs etc. Since this is such slow process I think it ideal for experimental cooks. You can learn quite a lot and produce some delicious food with this process.

Freezing

This is a very useful process for experimental cooks because many of you, I suspect, would be only a couple with one of you cooking for your spouse, or are living on your own. Either way, I find myself in a similar situation. Shopping for food in the supermarkets for one or two persons can be a problem. Some of the foods such as meats and some vegetables are packaged at an attractive price but the quantity is a lot more than you can use within the duration of its shelf life. You can deal with this in a number of ways. You can cook all of it in one go and freeze some for later use, or you can freeze the uncooked food. When freezing meats like sausages, bacon slices or chicken pieces the best way is to make smaller portions and wrap them or keep them apart in grease proof paper and put them back in the original pack and seal it in a freezer bag. This way you have the original instructions and you can take out what you need for the day without having to defrost the rest of it.

Freezing yogurt

By experimenting I have found that you can actually freeze yogurt. Best is to use the Greek type full fat yogurt. I found that the yogurt tubs that I bought could not be finished by the 'use by date' and were going bad. It is possible to keep the fresh yogurt a bit longer in the fridge if it is sealed properly and kept upside down rather than right way up. If some of the yogurt is frozen it will keep well but when defrosted it will turn into lovely butter milk with the fat particles floating above the watery part. This is excellent for making lassi (a lovely refreshing savoury drink) and some types of curries. However if you want the fat not to separate then try stirring the yogurt before freezing or even adding a couple of teaspoons of vodka which will reduce the crystallisation.

Freezing milk

Milk freezes well and if frozen on the day of purchase it can be kept for a couple of months. Make sure to use the supermarket plastic bottles and not glass bottles because the milk will expand on freezing and break the bottle. To defrost the milk take it out and leave it in the fridge or outside overnight. Shake it well before opening because the fat and the water will have separated.

Blanching

To freeze and preserve fresh vegetables you need to use a technique called blanching. The process of blanching stops the actions of the natural enzymes which can result in loss of flavour, colour and texture, and also cleans the surface removing dirt and organisms. Wash, clean and peel (if required) the vegetables and cut them into smaller pieces (ready for cooking when you defrost). In a large pan put ice into cold water to make ice-cold water. Boil water in another large pan, turn off the heat and immerse vegetables in this water for two to three minutes, drain them in a colander under cold tap water (to take the initial heat away) and put them immediately in the ice-cold water. Then drain, pack them in bags and freeze.

Poaching

Cooking delicate food like eggs and fish in water at a temperature of around 55°C is called poaching. For poaching eggs, heat salted water to just below boiling and slide the cracked egg in gently, cook for 3 to 5 minutes. Lift with a perforated spoon when cooked. Experimental cooks will find poaching eggs a simple method and worth trying. Only certain tender fish and shell fish are suitable for poaching. Fruits are poached in sugar syrup which retains the flavour and colour. You will need to cut the fruit first.

Special methods worth mentioning

Cooking in bags and foils

These are very easy ways to cook foods especially fish and meats and I recommend that experimental cooks have a go at it. All it takes is to prepare the meat (wash, rub with any marinades, spices or dressings, whatever you want) and wrap the prepared meat in a foil and bake it in the oven. The cooking bags are much the same except you put the food in it and any dry spice mix (often provided with the bag) and bake it as per instructions. Unless you overcook you can always produce delicious dishes using these methods. Remember that fish cooks quickly and is worth checking halfway through the cooking time to see if it is nearly ready.

Cooking with the lid on/off

Always cook food that has liquid or sauce in it with the lid on as the steam produced cooks the food thoroughly and quickly. For cooking all other foods like pulses, most of the vegetables etc. you will need to add a little water before putting the lid on. If you want the delicate green vegetables to keep their green colour, then do not use the lid while cooking.

Cooking with a wok

I recommend you try cooking with a wok. It is versatile, heats quickly to a high temperature and, although seen mainly in connection with cooking oriental food like noodles and stir-fry, you can use it for pretty much all kinds of cooking that require high heat. I use it for seasoning, frying onions, cooking vegetables etc. It is a one-pot method of cooking because after cooking one item you can simply set it aside in the serving bowl and cook the next item straight in the wok without having to wash it. Just wipe it with a tissue paper if you need to.

The other advantage is that while part of the items are cooking in the wok, you can tilt the wok and slide them out of the way and add some other items that need to be cooked separately on the heated part of the wok and then mix them together. This technique also allows you to add more seasoning if you have forgotten to do it in the beginning. The items put out of the way (on the rim side of the wok) will not burn or overcook while you are cooking other items in the centre part of the wok. It needs a bit of practice to do this. Another technique worth learning is to shake the wok and toss the food in it. You have probably seen this many times on TV cookery programmes. Make sure you get a wok that you can handle comfortably and that has a handle long enough to keep your hand away from the flames.

Moroccan tagine

This is a specially shaped pot that is used to cook succulent meats and stews. The shape of the pot traps the steam and thus retains the juices. It can be used in an oven or on a hob. The result is similar to that of a slow cooker but in a shorter time.

Hot oil seasoning

The term 'seasoning' in western cooking usually refers to adding salt, pepper, lemon juice, vinegars etc. to add flavour during the final part of cooking. This why I have used the term 'hot oil seasoning'. This is used in most Asian recipes. In fact almost all savoury food preparations begin with heating some sort of fat (oil, ghee etc.) in the pan and sprinkling in various aromatic ingredients. The most common are black mustard seeds, fenugreek seeds, asafoetida, red or green chillies, cumin seeds. This is an essential technique that adds all the traditional flavour to dishes, and experimental cooks should learn it. It is quite is simple to learn and we will describe it in detail in Section 10.

Cooking using a follow-on process

This simply means continuing the same process using a slightly different method. For example parboiling potatoes before frying or baking, or microwaving either before or after a part-cooking process such as finishing off the assembled biryani dish. This technique allows you to reduce the time or allows you to cook food such as potatoes so they are soft on the inside and crisp on the outside.

SUMMARY

1. Processes are different methods used for cooking. Some of these do not require application of heat.

2. Techniques are useful ways to improve the effectiveness of your cooking processes.

3. Many of the processes require preliminary preparation such as soaking, chopping etc.

4. It is important to learn and practise chopping onions and other vegetables properly and safely. The shape and size of the chopped food does alter the texture and the taste of your dish.

5. Marinating is a simple and useful process that adds flavour and is worth practising and experimenting with.

6. Controlling the heat is important for all the processes that require application of direct heat such as grilling, baking, deep or shallow frying. The food is still cooking even if the heat is turned off.

7. Preheat the oven to the required temperature before putting the item to bake. The higher shelf will be at a higher temperature than the lower. Place the food as directed in the recipe.

8. Slow cooking is one of the best and simplest ways to cook delicious curries and stews.

9. Freezing is one of the most useful processes for the experimental cook. You can use it to freeze smaller portions separated out from larger packs of meats, bacon, sausages etc.; and also freeze smaller portions of your own dishes for later use. Bread, milk and yogurt can be frozen.

10. Blanching is another useful process to preserve vegetables before freezing. You can freeze all sorts of vegetables, prepared and cut to size as you want.

PART II: THE ART OF COOKING

PRACTICE, VARIATIONS, AND CREATING YOUR OWN RECIPES

In Part I we have looked at our kitchen as a laboratory and our ingredients as chemicals. In this section we will look at cooking as an art. This is an important concept that all experimental cooks need to understand. The information provided in Part II and Part III is of a generic nature. Having understood a little bit of science behind the processes and the generic information about handling the processes you will be able to experiment and make your own variations. For example in Section 10 we will have a look at the basis of all curries and vegetable dishes and how you can make different combinations of these bases and sauces. You can use this to some extent for stews, goulash, pies and soups too. You do not need a strict recipe; you will see how you can experiment. You need not always start from scratch. In Section 9 you will learn how you can improve a dish or change one dish into another. This applies to your leftovers too. And if you make some mistakes it is generally possible to recover from having a complete disaster. You will see how in Section 8.

But of course you need some confidence and bit of a running start. So we will start with Section 7 that shows you how to make a few interesting dishes even if you have never cooked before.

Most of the recipes below require not much skill other than chopping, mixing and shallow or stir-frying or just using an oven or microwave. I suggest you select any that suits your taste or skill level and progress from there.

Remember that this is all about experimenting, so you do not need to follow any recipe exactly: do your own thing and experiment, which is what this book is all about.

Let me give you an analogy to explain my concept about showing how to cook this way. Suppose you want to learn to paint a picture with watercolours. Now if you have a picture to copy from, all the different tubes of the required colours and brushes and are then asked to copy the picture, what would be the result? Either you have some basic skills and create something looking vaguely like the original or you end up in a complete mess and give up. This is what happens to most people who are new to cooking, and are trying to follow recipes.

Continuing with my analogy of the watercolour; now instead if you have been first taught about the various types of papers and brushes to use, the types of paints and the pigments they are made from, how to mix them to create different colours and shades and brush techniques to achieve various effects, the result would turn out to be quite different. Agreed, your first picture will not be a work of art but most likely will be a passable one that you probably will be happy with; and what's more you will want to go on and practise more. In due course you will be enjoying your hobby and experimenting more with the techniques and paint more different, interesting pictures. Remember, in this analogy your pictures do not have to look like the one you are trying to copy. As long as you are happy with the result, that's what counts. My approach to experimental cooking is very similar to this. I know this works because I could not do any painting before but was taught this way and now I am enjoying my paintings.

Once you understand the basics and have tried your hand, then experiment and practise. Eventually you will not only be able to follow the recipes but will be able to make your own variations to suit your ingredients and your taste.

7

AN EASY START

A FEW SIMPLE DISHES THAT REQUIRE PRACTICALLY NO PREVIOUS COOKING EXPERIENCE

A brief note before you begin

The recipes in this section are really simple ideas about how you can cook simple dishes with no previous experience or cooking skills. They are neither classic nor original and, as you will notice, do not have exact quantities of ingredients. In fact there are suggested ingredients you can use but you can always experiment with any others you might think of.

The important thing is to create something that you like and tastes good. As regards taste, it is worth noting how we perceive taste and flavours. Although our tongue is the main organ via which we taste the food, the actual perception of the taste and flavours is a bit more complex than that. Our brain takes note of what signals we get from our tongue as well other senses such as sight, smell, touch (texture and temperature). The same food can taste different when some of these inputs change. The texture, the look of the dish and the temperature of the food for example makes considerable difference to how you perceive the final flavour. Food tastes different if you are suffering from a cold. The sense of taste varies from individual to individual.

There are six basic tastes that we play with when creating a recipe. These are sweet, sour, bitter, hot (chilli) and salty. Some regard umami (a sort of savoury, meaty taste) as another taste. Western cuisine does not regard hot as a separate taste but in Asian cuisine hot is regarded as a major taste and comes in a variety of flavours depending upon the ingredients. They come from the many ingredients that you will be using. You can try tempering one flavour with another such as sweet and bitter, sweet and hot, sour and salty and hot etc. Try experimenting with textures by adding crunchy things like croutons, nuts, seeds, sweetcorn, grated raw salads, noodles, steamed vegetables, sprouted beans etc. It is not a good idea to mix too many flavours or textures in the same dish. Quoting my analogy about water-colouring; mixing more than three colours usually ends up in a muddy colour. **Try to taste as you go; you can always add but cannot take away.**

After you have tried some of the recipes from this section, it may be also worthwhile to look at the techniques shown in the cookery programmes on TV. It is not important to follow the recipes: what you need is some more ideas to experiment with.

The easy start should give you some confidence in cooking the fun way. **But do not linger here**. Get adventurous, read through the 'Science of Cooking' section to understand a bit more about how the food cooks. This will allow you to be more experimental and also try any recipes from this book and other sources. Even when you do, it is important to know that any recipe is just a suggested idea. You can vary it with different ingredients and techniques according to your tastes, abilities and the ingredients you have available. **This is the essence of experimental cooking.**

The basic kit you should have

There is a lot of information in this book about the equipment and various ingredients that you will find useful. However you do not need everything at the start of your venture into cooking. Following is the list of items you will need in your basic kit to get started. You probably have most of what is listed and more.

Equipment

Two knives (one chef's knife and the other a smaller one): a chopping board: table place knives and forks and spoons (a fork is also useful as whisk): measuring spoons (tablespoon to teaspoon measures): one pint capacity measuring glass jar with millilitre and fraction of pint markings: baking tray for oven and grill: microwaveable glass bowls: a couple of cooking pots with lids: frying pan: a wok.

For your store cupboard

Spices like black pepper, salt, mustard seeds, cumin seeds, cumin and coriander powder, turmeric powder, garam masala, fresh garlic and root ginger, red chilli powder, red chilli flakes, tomato ketchup.

Other

Dark soya sauce, balsamic vinegar, tomato paste, mayonnaise, butter or margarine, eggs, packets of soups of your choice, rice noodles or egg noodles, cooking oil.

Starters

Prawn/ham cocktail

This is a quick, tasty and simple starter. You need:

❖ Cooked prawns, about two to three tablespoons per serving (Instead of cooked prawns you can use cooked ham like honey roast ham. If you prefer you can use both prawns and ham. If using ham chop it into bite size pieces).

❖ Chopped salad leaves (any will do), about a handful

❖ Mayonnaise for topping up as required

❖ Slice of lemon

❖ Seasoning like black pepper, salt, any sauce if you prefer like soya sauce, balsamic vinegar etc.

Ideally take a large wine glass. Mix the chopped salads, prawns and mayonnaise. Season with black pepper, salt to taste and any sauce if you like. Fill the glass. Add some more prawns or ham pieces on the top and serve with a slice of lemon.

It is possible to use crème fraîche or yogurt instead but it works best with mayonnaise.

Stuffed peppers

Cut some red/yellow/green peppers in half, clean them out, bake in the oven to make them a bit sweeter. Stuff them with prawns, mayonnaise, lettuce etc., similar to making the cocktail above. Another idea is to prepare the pepper casing as above and stuff them with spicy cooked prawns. (Cooked with ginger, garlic, a little chopped onion, chilli and salt to taste).

Salads

This is probably the simplest starter. All you need is a **few** of the following:

❖ Any type of salad leaves – wash and tear in smaller pieces or slice in strips with a knife. You can even use cabbage leaves if they are tender (or steam/microwave slightly to make them tender). Soaking the leaves in water for half an hour before use freshens up slightly stale leaves.

❖ Sliced tomatoes, cucumber.

❖ Grated carrots. You can slice them instead.

❖ Sliced celery. Slice it in thin slices for best flavour.

❖ Chopped onion (if you like).

❖ Sliced apple.

❖ Grated or chopped cheese.

❖ Separated Satsuma orange segments. I use the easy peel type, and slice off the edges to remove the rind.

❖ Nuts like peanuts, cashew nuts or seeds. I like pumpkin and sunflower seeds.

For dressing: Make a mixture in a small bowl from any of the following:

Mayonnaise, any sauces like soya sauce, vinegars, honey, lemon or lime juice, black pepper, salt to taste. There is more information on salad dressings in the later part of the book. Basically you need some sort of liquid ingredient such as oil, vinegar, or mayonnaise as your base in a small ramekin or dish and add to it any other flavours like lemon juice, honey, chilli flakes, garlic, soya sauce, chilli sauce, salt pepper etc. and pour over the salad and mix.

Chilli oil: This is really not a dressing as such but can be used in a variety of ways. You have probably seen this in Chinese restaurants. It is quite easy to make. Just heat about 125ml of oil (groundnut or sunflower, not rapeseed) to about the same temperature you do for frying. Do not let it overheat or boil. Let it cool completely, put it in a small bottle or jar. Add sliced very hot fresh chillies (red chillies, scotch bonnet, Thai chillies etc.). Leave to infuse for two three days. You can use it on top of any dish or use it as a dip.

Avocado salad

Cut the avocado in half and remove the stone. Serve on the top of your salads. You can fill the halves with prawns, pine nuts or finely chopped lettuce leaves and top it with mayonnaise for extra effect.

Raitas

Raitas are really side dishes or dips. The simplest one to make is using chopped tomatoes. Chop ripe tomatoes into small cubes, add some red chilli powder or chopped green chilli, crushed peanuts (optional), a pinch of sugar and a dash of lemon juice and salt to taste. Top it with yogurt and mix. You can use any other vegetables such as cucumber, grated carrots or even tender cabbage. Garnish with chopped coriander if available (or use fresh mint leaves).

Soups

You can make your own soups fairly easily; we will have a look at that later in the book. For now we will see how to use and improve readily available soups.

There are some wonderful and tasty packets of soup available in various stores. All you need is to add boiling water. But you can make it lot more interesting and tasty. Here is how.

There are lots of toppings that you can add. Simplest is grated cheese. A strong cheese like mature farmhouse Cheddar or Parmesan works best. Simply top your soup with it. If you are having French onion soup then top it with a real heap full and brown it under the grill till the cheese just starts melting. Enjoy it with plain or garlic toast.

Other toppings you can add are:

Spinach. I use frozen balls of spinach. Just take a couple of balls per cup, soften in the microwave for a couple of minutes so it is slightly cooked. Top your soup with it. This works best with clear and delicate soups.

Rice noodles. Choose the variety that just needs leaving in boiling water for a few minutes. You only need about one tablespoon per cup. Add on top of the hot bowl of soup.

Cooked crabmeat from the can. Fry the cooked meat to ensure it is cooked and hot. Mix it with your soup **and microwave the soup again before serving.**

Canned sweetcorn: The same as above, but boil the sweetcorn in the microwave for a couple of minutes till tender.

Seasoning: Use any seasoning of your choice like black pepper, any sauces like soya sauce, chilli sauce and salt to taste if needed.

Garlic toast

This is great with any soup or on its own. All you need is a slice of buttered toast. A thick slice of wholemeal bread works best. Crush a couple of cloves of garlic (no need to peel the skin off) and rub generously on the toast. Alternatively garlic purée is available in a tube. This is a good idea because it is even quicker and you can use the tube over a long time if kept in the fridge.

Garlic bread with mushrooms

Slice mushrooms in circular slices. Lightly sauté (lightly fry) them in butter, sprinkle salt and pepper and top up your garlic bread with them.

Snacks and light lunch

Toasted sandwiches with different fillings

Use your sandwich press or Panini press to make toasted sandwiches with different fillings. You should butter both sides of the bread slices before applying the filling.

Suggested fillings

Savoury: Ham, chutney, cheese, any leftover cooked meat (either thinly sliced or chopped), burgers (you will need to cook them before using by grilling or frying), peanut butter etc.

Sweet: My favourite is banana and peanut butter. Slice banana and mix with fair quantity (either equal to or even more than banana) of peanut butter (smooth or crunchy as per your choice), add a little sugar and black pepper to taste. Spread over buttered slices of bread, and toast in the sandwich press or under the grill.

Other fillings: Sultanas, honey, brown sugar, cooking chocolate, chocolate drops etc.

Cheese on toast

Lightly toast under the grill a thick slice of bread on one side only. Turn over and cover the top with grated cheese of your choice (add a little black pepper or red chilli powder for extra kick) and toast till the cheese melts. Delicious with soups.

Baked potato variations

This is best done in a microwave oven. Clean a large baking potato (leave skin on), prick the skin in a few places with a fork. Place in a little water in a bowl and bake for 10 to 12 minutes according to the size of the potato, making sure that all the water has not boiled off. Check if cooked by piercing with a fork.

Cut the potato in half and place a knob of butter on each half. Sprinkle with salt and pepper.

Fillings: You can have a variety of fillings such as salad leaves, cheese, tomato or cucumber slices, chopped ham, prawns, tuna meat, onion rings etc. For seasoning you can use tomato ketchup, hot sauces, mustard, horseradish etc.

Burgers

Use ready-made beef, chicken or lamb burgers. You can either use burger buns, or rolls or crumpets, spread with mayonnaise or crème fraîche. For filling you can use salad leaves or cheese.

Spicy omelette

For a basic omelette use two eggs per person. Whisk the eggs in a bowl and add seasoning such as salt and pepper and fry with little oil in a frying pan covering the pan for just a minute or two till one side is cooked then turn over and cook the other side with or without covering the pan.

For a spicy omelette add finely chopped onion, chopped green chilli (or red chilli powder), sliced tomato pieces and some cheese. You can add some chopped coriander if you like. Try any other herbs if you prefer.

Serve with a fresh slice of buttered bread or in a wrap.

Egg fried breads, savoury and sweet

Whisk a couple of eggs in a bowl large enough to dip a slice of bread.

For savoury bread season with salt, pepper or chilli (chopped garlic or cheese if you wish).

For sweet bread, flavour with honey or brown sugar and sultanas.

Dip and coat both sides and shallow fry with a little oil (or butter if you wish) with the lid on till both sides are nicely brown.

Meals

Fried sausages with baked beans and onion gravy

Shallow fry or oven cook the sausages. (If cooking in the oven just brush the sausages with oil and place in a baking tray). For onion gravy, finely slice some onions, fry them in the oil leftover from shallow frying the sausages (for extra flavour) till golden brown and soft, add soya sauce to make gravy to your required consistency. Season with black pepper and salt if required (taste before adding salt). Serve with simmered baked beans and chips.

Sausage stir-fry

This is really a simple, healthy and delicious dish. It works better with chipolatas. Lightly shallow fry the chipolatas till light brown and almost cooked, ensuring that you do not fully cook (as you are going to cook them again). Cut them into smaller pieces. Roughly chop pak choi (also known as bok choi) or tender cabbage, although it works better with pak choi. Add sliced garlic and finely sliced ginger to hot oil in a pan or wok and cook the vegetables for a couple of minutes. Then add the cooked chipolatas and 1 to 1½ tbsp of soya sauce to coat the vegetables and chipolatas. Cook for a couple of minutes. Season with black pepper and salt if required.

Baked fish in foil with peas or sweetcorn

This works best with cod or salmon. I use cod loins which are nice fleshy steaks, or boneless salmon steak. Wash the fish, make a few slashes on the surface with a knife to absorb the seasoning.

Make a mixture of spices to rub into the fish. You can use anything like salt, black pepper, garlic purée, ginger, soya sauce, lemon juice. Taste the mixture as you go along before you use it so that you can adjust the flavour. (I use garlic and ginger paste and chilli powder with any garam masala, but it works just as well with just black pepper, salt and lemon juice rubbed into it.)

Place the fish on an aluminium baking foil and rub the mixture into it, coating both sides. Wrap the fish into a parcel and bake in the oven at medium temperature till cooked. Fish cooks in a short time so do not overcook it. If the flesh has started flaking it is cooked. Depending upon the size, it normally should not take more than 12 to 15 minutes at about 150 to 160°C (gas mark 4 to 5). Serve with canned peas or sweetcorn.

Chicken cooked in foil or roasting bag with potato wedges

This is similar to cooking the fish as described above, except you use chicken (leg, wings or half chicken, anything except breast which is too tender to cook this way). You can either use foil or a roasting bag.

With a roasting bag you will need to make a dry spice mix. You can get roasting bags with the spice in a sachet supplied in which case all you need to do is place the chicken in the bag, add the spices and shake it to cover. You can do the same with your own dry spice mixture. With the roasting bag follow the instructions for temperature and time that comes with it.

Chicken requires a higher temperature (about 180°C) and longer time than fish: about 30 minutes. You can see it is fully cooked when the juices run clear when the bird is pierced in the thigh with a skewer.

Potato wedges: You can either use ready-made wedges or make your own. To make your own, clean and peel potatoes, slice into wedges, mix some olive oil, garlic purée, salt and pepper in a small bowl and coat the wedges with the mixture.

Either way place the wedges in a baking tray and bake at about 180°C till golden brown. You can do this along with the chicken at the same time. Serve with tomato ketchup or barbecue sauce.

Gammon and pineapple with chips

Oven bake the gammon slices in a baking tray with pineapple slices covered with a little pineapple juice till the gammon is cooked and the pineapple slices are a little brown. For temperature and timing see instructions on the packet. It usually takes about 20 minutes at 190°C or gas mark 5. Serve with potato chips or wedges.

Spicy couscous

This is one of the easiest dishes to make. Basically couscous is a variety of semolina. You get pre-cooked couscous that only requires you to add boiling water, the instructions are always on the packet. To make spicy couscous, make the spicy mixture in advance. You can use a variety of vegetables, leftover meat etc. I like to use sliced red and orange peppers and spring onions and a couple of green chillies cooked with sliced garlic, and ginger and seasoned with salt to taste. Couscous is a great accompaniment to have with any meat dish instead of rice. For garnish, try Moroccan mint. The addition of a couple of knobs of butter makes it deliciously moist and tasty. You can experiment a lot with couscous without doing much cooking.

Chow Mein

Chow Mein means stir-fried noodles. It can be made using meat, fish or pork. You can also use your leftover vegetables or meat such as cooked lamb, pork or chicken. Thinly slice any vegetables or meat. If using uncooked meat, marinate the meat in light soya sauce and some white wine or rice wine and salt and pepper before stir-frying.

For noodles, egg noodles or rice noodles are best. Look for the instructions on the packet about cooking the noodles. Egg noodles need boiling for four to five minutes and for rice noodles you need to pour boiling water on them and leave them to stand for four to five minutes in a bowl, then immerse them in cold water to cool.

To stir-fry you will need a wok, sliced garlic and sliced ginger, salt, pepper and dark soy sauce or a sachet of ready-made frying sauce. The wok should be very hot before adding a little oil. When the oil just starts smoking add the ginger, garlic, the vegetables or meat or the mixture of the two and stir it to cook (avoid overcooking). Then add the noodles and soy sauce, or ready-made sauce and a little sesame oil if you have, and any seasoning. Stir-fry for half a minute or so and it should be ready.

Rice noodle variations

This is an even more simplified version of a sort of Chow Mein. Just use rice noodles to add to your leftovers and do a stir-fry.

Rice noodles are quite handy and easy to cook because they only need to be placed in boiling water without actually cooking them. You can add rice noodles to all kinds of vegetables such as peas, sweetcorn, courgettes, or to any leftover meat or vegetable dishes. Try using different kinds of spices, sauces or soya sauce.

Side vegetables

Spicy spinach

Use leaf spinach either fresh or frozen. The frozen variety comes in balls about golf ball size. This is more convenient for making a small quantity because you can use just a few balls from the packet. Defrost the spinach if frozen. If using fresh spinach wash and drain and roughly chop in large chunks. If using baby spinach you do not need to chop it. Heat oil in a pan or a wok, add plenty of sliced garlic cloves and a couple of green chillies or dried red chillies and a pinch of salt. Add the spinach when garlic just starts to get brownish (do not let it burn). Stir for two three minutes and turn off the heat. Do not cover the pan because it will generate liquid. Do not overcook.

This is a quick, tasty and simple dish and goes well with any meat or curry dishes.

Spicy sweetcorn

Use canned sweetcorn. It does not require much cooking. The method is virtually similar to that of spinach except add some chopped spring onions or normal onions. As per spinach add garlic and chillies to hot oil, add onion and cook till pink. Add the sweetcorn and a tablespoon of water, cover and cook for a few minutes till sweetcorn is tender but not overcooked.

Peas

Same as sweetcorn, use frozen peas, no need to defrost. Use chopped spring onion or normal onion. Add some finely chopped garden mint or Moroccan mint while peas are cooking. Cook with lid on. Do not overcook, it should take only a couple of minutes for the peas to cook.

Desserts

Banana dessert with milk/yogurt/custard/ice cream

Slice and slightly crush the banana. Add milk and any essence such as vanilla, orange. Add brown sugar to taste and leave in the fridge to cool. You can also use yogurt, custard or ice cream instead of milk. For added flavour top up with peeled satsuma slices.

Fruit yogurt

Same as the banana dish except use canned fruit in yogurt.

Fruit salad

Same as above except use tinned fruit with custard. Use ready-made custard, a lot easier than making your own.

Fruit trifle

Same as the fruit salad except add it on top of a plain cake such as sponge cake, or any simple cake you may have. You can even try using some soft biscuits similar to Jaffa Cakes. Top it with some ice cream when serving.

Top up with a couple of teaspoons of orange or cherry liqueur for a real treat. You also can try cherry brandy or similar alcoholic drink.

Try crushed nuts as an additional topping if you like a crunchy texture.

8

DISASTER RECOVERY

Mistakes are not a waste of time. They also serve as a way of learning the processes, what went wrong and why. Sometimes you might end up creating new dish but, as the saying goes, 'prevention is better than cure'. You can prevent your dish going too far the wrong way by following these simple rules.

1. Think ahead about what ingredients you are going to use and in particular what seasoning you will be using. Put aside small amounts of your seasoning ingredients in separate small plates or bowls.

2. Now you have a rough idea of the proportion of various items you are thinking of. Remember some flavours complement each other but others produce contrasting results. If in doubt taste them.

3. Think about the order in which you will add them during the cooking process. In most cases you can add a smaller quantity and add any more if necessary after tasting the food. **You can always add more but cannot take away.**

4. Try avoiding the temptation of adding too many different seasoning ingredients especially in larger quantity.

5. When you think you have achieved a reasonably acceptable taste, stand back and leave it alone; do not keep adjusting the flavour. The only minor adjustment you should make is slowly adding one or two of the same ingredients that are already in the dish and tasting as you go. Remember it may take a few seconds for the effect to take place. My

watercolour instructor always reminded me that when your picture is looking reasonably OK, it is time to stand back, do not keep going over again and again! It is the same with cooking.

6. Do not let your food burn. Be mindful of what you are cooking. It may help to use a kitchen timer to remind you.

Mistakes are of two types, omission and commission.

Mistakes of omission

If you forgot to add an ingredient to curries or stews or sauces in many cases you can add it and reheat the food. Before taking any corrective action taste the food: if it is OK then leave it as it is.

If you forgot to do a process on the ingredient that you have not yet added, again in most cases you can carry out a separate process on that ingredient and add to the main dish. For example frying onion or adding a vegetable.

Mistakes of commission

These usually present a problem, like adding too much salt, sugar, vinegar or chilli.

One way to deal with this is to add more of the **main ingredient**; in other words make a larger quantity (if you have more left) so the resulting taste would come out about right again. You can try freezing the additional quantity, or why not share with your friends or neighbours?

To neutralise the unwanted flavours you can try the

following:

Salt: It is difficult to take away a too salty taste. Remedies include adding more water (if the dish is liquid), adding sugar, or a little acidic taste like lemon or vinegar.

Chilli: Add some sugar or any bland ingredient. If the dish has gravy, try yogurt or milk or cream. Who knows, you might end up in inventing a new dish!

Sweet: Try adding either chilli or an acidic flavour if the dish is savoury. If it is a sweet dish then try milk, yogurt or add more of the main ingredients.

Bitter: Try adding sugar or any acidic flavour.

Sour: Either make it into a sweet and sour flavour by adding chilli sauce or dissolve a little sodium bicarbonate in water and heat the food, it will froth indicating the reaction of the soda.

Another way to save your dish

It may be possible that you can change your dish into something else altogether. I call this morphing and is covered in the next section.

Burnt dish and pan

If the dish is burnt beyond any use then you can do nothing except throw it away. If your pan is burnt then you can clean it by the following method:

Keep the pan dry and take the worst off by gently scraping away the burnt food. Make a thick paste of baking soda (sodium bicarbonate) in water. Cover the burnt area generously and leave for at least twelve hours. Then clean the dried paste with a paper tissue and brush the pan with a hard brush with a little hot water (do not flood the pan). Then, using a scouring pad, try clearing any residues left. Sometimes you might have to repeat this process.

9

ABOUT MORPHING

Morphing is changing one thing into something else. This is a useful technique for experimental cooks because by morphing you can use something that you have already cooked or bought in the shop or got in a takeaway meal that you find uninteresting. You can change the taste or texture or make it into altogether different dish.

Here are a few ideas: remember the starting point could be a dish that you already have, it could be a leftover dish because you cooked a larger quantity and do not wish to eat it a second time, or a dish you have bought from the shops or got from a takeaway that you find is too bland or not to your liking.

IMPORTANT NOTE WHEN USING LEFTOVERS:

The leftovers should be properly covered and stored in a fridge. Do not leave them for more than a couple of days. Check the condition before using. Any leftovers should be cooked thoroughly.

Stir-fried dishes

You can change stir-fry meat like pork or lamb into curry or sort of patties. For curry, cook some chopped onion in whatever spices you want. Chop the stir-fried meat and add to the onion. If you have a little green spinach available add it too. For gravy, add a little water or you can make some gravy using stock cubes or gravy granules. For patties, mix together finely chopped onion, a little chilli, a little garam masala and the chopped meat. Make flat cakes. Roll them in breadcrumbs, then in beaten egg and again in breadcrumbs and shallow fry.

You can also try to make shepherd's pie or use the meat in a wrap.

Combine with leftover rice to make a kind of biryani dish.

Leftover meat curry

Here you can do the reverse of the above. Use it for stir-fry, patties, shepherd's pie etc.

Combine with leftover rice to make a kind of biryani dish.

Leftover meat is excellent for adding to soups especially if you are using a slow cooker. Chop it finely and add to the soup towards the end, enough to form gravy but do not overcook.

If there is a lot of meat you can make excellent clear soup. Drain away the gravy. Chop the meat into about 5mm pieces. Fry the pieces in a little onion for a couple of minutes. Add any finely chopped vegetables like carrots or celery. Make the soup in the usual way, then strain the clear liquid.

Rice

Rice is so versatile that you can always make something else out of it. For more information about cooking and keeping rice refer to Part III. Properly cooked rice can be used again; I do it all the time. Excess plain rice can be converted into savoury rice, meat biryani, fried rice, vegetable pilaf – the list is endless. Refer to Chapter 12 for details.

Vegetables

Any vegetables that you did not like the taste of or that are left over are excellent to add to the soup. Do not add too large a quantity, so as not to drown the taste of your soup.

Soups

You may not like the taste of some of the quick soup packets. You can either use them as an addition to your home-made soups or make the soup from the packet and 'jazz' it up by adding other ingredients such as grated cheese, paprika powder, soya sauce, steamed spinach (or a couple of balls of frozen spinach cooked for a minute in the microwave), sweetcorn, crabmeat, noodles, cooked prawns etc.

Mashed potatoes

Like rice, potato is a versatile ingredient. There are so many things you can do with potato. Refer to Chapter 13 for details. You can combine it with leftover meat or vegetables to make a pie or mix together a spicy potato rosti with chopped onion, green chilli and coriander shallow fried in a pan.

Fish

Fried or baked fish is ideal or converting into spicy fish cakes. The method is similar to that for meat patties.

Crumpet:

Toast with cheese sprinkled with black pepper. Use as sandwich with ham, spam, chutney, coleslaw etc.

An example of morphing

This is something I did recently and it illustrates my point about morphing. I had some leftover gammon and pineapple from the previous night. The next day I made tasty stir-fry for my lunch. I placed a small amount of rice noodles in hot water. Then I finely sliced some tender romaine lettuce and spring onions, some garlic and ginger and also the leftover gammon and pineapple slices. First I added garlic and ginger and one whole red dried chilli to the hot oil in the wok, tossed in the sliced gammon, cooked it for a couple of minutes then added the sliced pineapple and then the rest of the ingredients. To finish off I added the rice noodles and some dark soya sauce. It was a deliciously sweet and hot Chow Mein.

10

MAKING THE BASIC SPICE MIXTURES FOR ALL CURRIES AND VEGETABLES

In this section we will look at the various combinations of spices and marinades that are used in most Asian meat and vegetarian dishes. You can also use these for western dishes like stews, goulash, soups etc. with minor changes. Western dishes are a little less spicy, so you will need only a few of the spices, and in smaller quantities. There is usually black pepper instead of hot chilli powder.

As you have noticed I have kept the information on the actual cooking processes of meats and vegetables separate from the information on spice mixes and marinades. This is deliberate. There are a variety of combinations of masala mixes which are used in various Asian recipes. If you look at the recipes of various Asian dishes you will find that many of the spices occur in similar combinations of these mixes with some extra ingredients in some cases. This is the way that chefs experiment and create their recipes.

As an experimental cook if you have information on some essential mixes and if you know the basic process of cooking various meats and vegetables, you can experiment with them and create your own recipes or follow others' ideas without actually having to follow a particular recipe exactly. This is a lot simpler process to learn cooking. For example if you come across an interesting dish in a restaurant or at your friend's place or see it being cooked on TV, you will get a basic idea about how to recreate something similar. This is the way my dear wife taught me and it worked for me very well. I am sure it will work for you too. Always remember: cooking is a matter of practice; if you do not achieve the desired result, think of how it could be improved and try again. Keep a note of what you are doing; it will help you to analyse your success or failure. When you achieve your desired result you'll have a written recipe!

Important note about using spices

Remember that spices are generally used for **enhancing** the natural flavours of the food and **not to drown them**, just like in a painting using too many colours confuses the observer and reduces the freshness of the appearance of the painting.

The spices you will need

The complete list of useful spices and their description is given at the end of this section. However the few essential spices required for the basic mixes are listed below. Refer to the list of spices for information about their use before trying any basic spice mixture. These are:

Asafoetida, black pepper, chilli flakes, cloves, coriander powder, cumin powder, garlic, mustard seeds, whole dried red chilli, root ginger, turmeric.

Cooking onion and smoking techniques: See notes at the end of this section.

Basic mixtures for vegetable dishes (side vegetables, curries and rice etc.)

Using the bases included in this section, you will be able to experiment with various vegetables, such as leaf vegetables like spinach, cabbage and broccoli, or root vegetables like potatoes or carrots, or other marrow type vegetables like courgettes. You will be able to cook vegetable curries, all types of rice, and other savoury dishes using semolina, couscous etc.

Each type of mixture details the ingredients and information on what kind of dishes it is best suited to, however you can explore other uses. The relative proportion of the various ingredients is approximate and based on two servings. In most cases the quantities are not too critical and you can use a little more or a little less. Some ingredients which I have singled out should be used with extra care because using too much may spoil the taste. In any case, until you become familiar with them, it is best to use a little less rather than a little more.

All seasoning is added to hot oil in a pan or wok. The oil should be quite hot so that the ingredients start reacting straight away. The Basic seasoning is described first, followed by information on how to incorporate it in typical dishes.

Type 1. Simple basic seasoning for all purposes (vegetables and savoury rice)

You can get away with using this mixture most of the time for most Asian dishes. For variation refer to type 4 base.

To hot oil add first black mustard seeds (about 2 tsps); as soon as they start popping up reduce the heat, do not let it burn and add the rest of the ingredients.

EXAMPLE 1: Using type 1 for vegetable dishes without onion
Useful for all kinds of vegetables like spinach, cabbage, courgettes.

Chop the vegetables, make the seasoning as shown above and add the vegetables to the hot pan of seasoning. Add turmeric (¾ to 1 tsp: do not overdo), cumin powder (½ tsp), coriander powder (½ to 1 tsp), chilli powder and salt to taste. Add a couple of tablespoons of water and cook, lid on except for leafy green vegetables like spinach. Normally you do not need to add any water to spinach.

EXAMPLE 2: Using type 1 for vegetables with chopped onion:
Virtually the same as above except add chopped onion first to the seasoning in the pan, cook the onion then add the rest of the spices as in Example 1 above and then add the vegetables. This method is often used to make the dish with a little sauce. For this add a bit more water and cook with the lid on. You can make spicy potatoes or aubergine with sauce this way. Optional additions: chopped tomatoes, whole green chilli, tomato purée, cinnamon and clove

powder for extra kick.

EXAMPLE 3: Using type 1 for savoury rice with or without onions
Same as above except use pre-cooked rice instead of vegetables.

Type 2. Simple base with cumin seeds with ghee or oil.

This is a very simple and useful base for seasoning. This works best with ghee (clarified butter) but you can use cooking oil instead if you prefer. Simply heat 1 to 1½ tbsp of ghee (or oil). Wait till it is fairly hot, add about 1 to 1½ tbsp of cumin seeds. They will start becoming dark in a few seconds, do not let them burn; add other ingredients (see below) and stir and cook.

EXAMPLE 1: Using type 2 base for vegetables
Spicy dry potatoes: Peel and cut potatoes into small (approximately 1cm) cubes. (Do not have larger cubes as they will not cook quickly with this method). Add these to the type 2 base as soon as the cumin seeds are turning dark. Add black pepper or red chilli powder or whole dried red chillies. Stir for a few seconds and cover. The potatoes will cook in the steam generated. Check, and if needed add a tablespoon of water to create more steam. Add salt to taste. This is a dry dish. This also works well with other root vegetables and marrow type vegetables like courgettes. (It will not work well if you add chopped onions.) You can also cook pumpkins this way, but cut the pumpkin into about

one inch cubes otherwise they will turn soft and liquid.

EXAMPLE 2: Using type 2 base for grated savoury potato

We will cover this recipe in detail in Chapter 22. Grate potatoes, soak in cold water to take out some of the starch, drain, squeeze and let them dry for an hour or so. (You can leave out this step and use the grated potatoes as they are, but they become slightly sticky during the cooking). Crush peanuts by pounding (you need about one tenth of the volume of the grated potatoes). First, add to the hot base some green sliced chillies, then add the grated potatoes, cook for a couple of minutes, add some salt (careful if you are using salted peanuts), add the crushed roasted peanuts, cover and cook. Check later, and if necessary add a tablespoon of water to generate more steam. Serve with a slice of lemon. This also works very well with sweet potato.

Type 3. Garlic base

This method is very similar to the Type 2 base but instead of cumin seeds use sliced or crushed garlic cloves. You need plenty of them – at least 1½ to 2 tbsp. This method is particularly useful for cooking leaf vegetables, mushrooms, aubergine and pak choi. It is also the base for simple stir-fry vegetables.

EXAMPLE 1: Using type 3 base for vegetables.

Aubergine: Cut aubergines into 1 cm (½ inch) pieces. You need a bit more oil for this recipe. To the type 3 base (while hot), add whole dried red chillies or green chillies, add the aubergine pieces, put the lid on and cook for a few minutes, then add chopped tomatoes and salt to taste and a teaspoon of jaggery (or sugar). Cook further. You can also try adding a little vinegar to produce a sweet and sour taste. If you prefer you can add some water to have a little sauce. Garnish with chopped coriander.

Stir-fry mushrooms: Prepare the type 3 base in a wok, ensure it is quite hot. Add whole small button mushrooms or sliced mushrooms. Shake the wok, do not stir too much and do not cover. Add black pepper and salt to taste. Delicious as a side dish with baked or grilled meat or fish dishes.

Type 4. Most popular base with mustard seeds, asafoetida.

If you want to know just one recipe for the base, I would say this is the one. I have deliberately listed it after the others because it involves using asafoetida (refer to the list of spices in this section). It is quite easy to obtain. You will find it in most supermarkets and certainly in ethnic grocery shops. It is sold as a pungent yellow powder in small cans or bottles. You only need a small pinch or two (less than ¼ tsp). This base has only two basic ingredients: mustard seeds and asafoetida.

To very hot oil add two to three teaspoons of mustard seeds. As soon as they start popping add the asafoetida, then add the rest of the vegetables and ingredients. If you are worried about burning the seasoning, turn off the heat then add the other ingredients, stir and **immediately** put the heat on. You then add about ¼ to ½ tsp of turmeric powder and cook. Chilli powder can be added to the mix or you can put whole red or green chilli along with the mustard seeds at the beginning. Normally garlic is not used with this type of base. If you want to use onion, add chopped onion to the base and cook it before you add the rest of the vegetables (see examples).

EXAMPLE 1: Using type 4 base

Spicy potato: Peel and cut three or four medium size potatoes into 2 cm (¾ inch) cubes. Thinly slice one medium size onion. Make the type 4 base as above, add the onion and cook till soft. Add red chilli powder, about ¾ tsp of cumin powder and 1½ tsps of coriander powder, any garam masala (optional) and turmeric powder. (If adding garam masala, either use less cumin and coriander powder or omit them altogether). Add the potatoes, then stir and cook for three or four minutes. Add about two to three tablespoons of water and cook with the lid on till the potatoes are soft. Add salt to taste and some lemon juice. If you need any more heat sprinkle some chilli flakes. If you prefer soft vegetables (like you see in take away foods) slightly crush the potatoes and cook a little longer. Garnish with chopped coriander.

You can make aubergines also the same way. Add 1 tsp of jaggery or sugar to temper the bitter flavour of aubergines.

Savoury Rice: See detailed information on cooking rice in the recipe section.

Make the base as above. Use only a small amount of asafoetida or leave it out altogether. Add a whole dried red chilli to the base. Optionally you can add some raw peanuts (not roasted). Then add the soaked rice to the base. Add salt to taste. You do not need turmeric here, but can add some if you prefer. This is a good recipe for the experimental cook. You can add any vegetables, sweetcorn etc. to make it into special vegetable rice. You can eat it on its own without any side dish or curry.

Type 5. South Indian base using curry leaves, urid daal and red whole chilli or black pepper.

This is a less spicy base with a delicate flavour that can be used with most vegetables and also in South Indian type semolina-based dishes. The base is very simple. To a tablespoon of hot oil add two whole dried red chillies or a tablespoon of whole black peppercorns, a couple of tablespoons of urid daal (unsoaked) and a tablespoon of fresh or dried curry leaves (fresh leaves will give better flavour). The daal will start getting pink and then light brown. Add other ingredients to the hot mixture. If you are concerned about burning the daal, turn off the heat and add the ingredients and then turn the heat on again immediately.

EXAMPLE 1: type 5 base for making savoury semolina
Note regarding semolina: The actual amount of water absorbed in the semolina during the cooking depends on the type of semolina and how much you have browned it. The amount given here is a guide: you may require more or less.

For two servings take about 75g of coarse semolina (you can

use fine if coarse is unavailable), one medium onion coarsely chopped (not too rough) and a couple of whole dried red chillies. First dry fry the semolina till it changes colour to pink to light brown, but stop before it starts turning a dark colour; set aside. Make the type 5 base, add chopped onion and cook till soft and pink and set aside. Boil water (about three to four times the volume of semolina) and keep it ready. Add the semolina to the cooked onion base and cook for a couple of minutes, add salt to taste, add about ¼ of the hot water, cook and stir well for a few minutes, then add more water in **small amounts at a time**, and **keep stirring.** The semolina will start swelling as it cooks. Keep adding water, stop just when it starts to form lumps. You will probably need at least ¾ of the water you have boiled (equal to about three times the volume of semolina). Best to stop little early, taste to see if it is cooked and soft then add a little water at a time till it is done. Put the lid on and cook on low heat for up to 10 minutes to finish off. The semolina should be soft and would have small globules but should not be a sticky mess. Adding a little butter at the end will make it richer and creamy and will help to separate the granules. You can increase the hotness by sprinkling it with chilli flakes. Serve with a twist of lemon.

Type 6. Marinade cum paste for meats

This is the most common marinade for meats and fish for curries, and also for baking. There are options and variations, but following is the general idea with some suggested options. This is again a good area for the experimental cook to try especially for baking and pan frying meats. In addition to the spices and ingredients mentioned in this type, there are many ready-made pastes and mixes available which can be used with this type of method.

Basic mixture: Use ginger and garlic paste (about 40% ginger and 60% garlic). If you are using it often it is better to make some and bottle it and keep it in the fridge where it will last for two three months. It also can be frozen.

In a bowl make the mixture: You will need about two to three teaspoons of the ginger garlic paste (depending upon the quantity of meat). A little more or less will not spoil the taste. To this add some yogurt and red chilli powder. **If you are using a ready-made curry or tandoori paste then stop here and use the paste with the instructions provided.**

If you are not using a ready-made paste then continue: To the above add ½ a tsp of turmeric, ½ a tsp of cumin powder, 1 tsp of coriander powder, a little garam masala (optional) and a little lemon juice. Mix all together.

Optional extras: You can try tomato paste, dark soya sauce, chilli sauce (instead of chilli powder).

EXAMPLE 1: Using the type 6 marinade.
Baking meats: Coat the meat pieces in marinade. Leave for a couple of hours then bake in the oven at the recommended temperature. Wrap in cooking foil to keep it moist. Brown the surface without foil if you want the outside crisp.

Grilling: Prepare as above except do not use foil.

Making curries: coat the meat or fish in the marinade. Leave for a couple of hours. To make curry, heat about one tablespoon oil or ghee in a pan, add any extras if you wish (see list below), add finely chopped onion, cook it till soft. Add the meat pieces and stir them around for a couple of minutes to brown the surface making sure that the marinade is not burning. Add some water, cover and cook. Check when the meat is nearly cooked, add salt to taste and adjust the water to your requirements and cook the meat till tender.

Optional extras for curries

To be added before adding onion: (small quantities): cloves, cinnamon sticks, whole black pepper, pounded mixture of roasted whole coriander seeds, cloves and cinnamon.

To be added during or after the cooking: cinnamon powder, clove powder, tomato paste, tomato ketchup.

List of spices you will need

Most of the items listed below are in common use, though not in the same recipe. The items listed below are the minimum you need. I suggest you stock those to start with and add the rest as you progress. The items marked by two asterisks (**) are useful additions but are used only occasionally. You might think that it is a lot of items but together they will allow you to make many combinations of mixes. It is similar to having to buy certain tubes of paint before you can experiment with watercolour. You can buy most of the spices from good supermarkets. The best place to buy is ethnic grocery shops where you will get better value for your money.

Asafoetida. A yellow powder with very strong smell available in small containers. It is the dried and ground resin of a certain plant. It is used in **very small** quantity (usually about a pinch or two). Normally it is added to hot oil just after adding mustard seeds. It is important to ensure that it does not burn. The best way to do that is to turn the heat off and immediately add the asafoetida, then resume cooking by adding other items.

Black pepper. Can be used in place of chilli or in combination with chilli.

Chilli flakes. Chilli flakes contain intense flavour. They can be used to top up the hot flavour of a dish. Added to dry savoury dishes they give intense bursts of hot flavour as you eat. Added to chocolate bases in sweet dishes they give a unique flavour to the sweetness which you only feel as an aftertaste as you eat. Something interesting for experimental cooks to try.

Cinnamon. Dried inner bark of the cinnamon tree, available as sticks. Thin long sticks are more flavoursome. It has a hot and sweet aroma, and is used in many curry dishes and savoury rice dishes. It is added to hot oil as a seasoning or added to rice while boiling.

Ground cinnamon and clove powder. A ready-made

mix of ground cinnamon and cloves is quite handy to add to savoury dishes (the proportion is one part cloves to about three or four parts of cinnamon). This should not be added to hot oil as seasoning. Add it to the main ingredients during cooking or just before it is ready. This adds distinctive flavour and aroma to dishes cooked with semolina, cracked wheat and also sauces for curries. Sprinkle a small amount on dry savoury dishes or curries and side vegetables to give that extra kick.

Citric acid. This has a strong acidic, lemon-like taste and can be used instead of lemon or lemon juice. Citric acid is quite useful when you want to add acidity to a dry dish without making it soggy. It is also used to give bursts of acid flavours during eating.

Cloves. Buds of the clove tree. Cloves have a hot and slightly bitter taste. Used as seasoning by adding to hot oil, also to rice and sweet dishes as aromatic flavouring.

Coriander powder. Powder made from ground coriander seeds. It has a pungent and citrus-like flavour. It is one of the most common items used in almost all curry and vegetable and lentil dishes. It is usually added to the onion or vegetables during the cooking process, or while the sauce is simmering. Used also in a marinade along with other spices mixed with yogurt.

Coriander seeds. Seeds of the popular coriander plant. Have a lovely pungent flavour. When dry roasted and pounded they release a lovey oily aromatic flavour. (See cumin seeds).

Cumin powder. Ground cumin seeds. It has a strong and distinctive flavour. The strength depends upon where the cumin seeds came from. Certain cumin seeds, like those from Morocco, are very strong. Use only a small quantity. The most common item used in conjunction with coriander powder. For each teaspoon of coriander powder use only half a teaspoon of cumin powder.

Cumin seeds. These are small grass-like seeds. They come in variety of colours from light green, dark green to brownish. The most commonly used item for seasoning in hot oil. Cumin gives a lovely pungent flavour when used on its own and added to hot ghee, oil or butter for making delicately flavoured savoury dishes with potato, sago, sweet potato etc. Cumin seeds are often dry roasted with coriander seeds and pounded (not ground) which releases the aromatic oil. This mixture is much more aromatic than using a mixture of cumin and coriander powders. The experimental cook should try it sometime.

Fennel seeds. ★★ Have an aromatic aniseed flavour. Can add to hot oil but usually dry roasted and slightly crushed and added to meat dishes, soups, stews etc. to give lovely sweet and aromatic flavour. You can eat the seeds as a mouth freshener after your meal.

Fenugreek seeds. ★★ These are small dried seeds with a **bitter** and pungent aroma. Used as seasoning in hot oil. Adds flavour to bland vegetables like cabbage. **Use only**

one to three seeds.

Garlic. Very commonly used in Asian as well as Western cuisine. Sliced or crushed cloves are added to hot oil as seasoning. As a paste (normally together with ginger paste) it is used for cooking all kinds of vegetables and meats. Great for cooking mushrooms in butter or cooking steaks. Garlic paste makes lovely garlic bread.

Garlic and ginger paste: Make paste using garlic and root ginger in roughly 60:40 ratio (you can adjust the ratio a little according to your taste). You can keep in fridge for a few weeks or freeze it. **Very useful** for all meat and vegetable dishes and for marinades.

Ghee. ★★ Ghee is clarified butter and has a lovely grainy texture. It is used instead of butter in many Asian recipes. Some may find the taste of ghee on its own a bit rancid. However once you have added it to the food you do not have that kind of taste. It imparts a lovely rich creamy taste to food that is superior to butter. Ghee is better suited for seasoning food with cumin seeds than oil. Small cans of pure ghee are available.

Jaggery. ★★ Jaggery is unrefined sugar made from cane sugar juice. It is very commonly used in India for cooking all sorts of dishes instead of refined sugar. It is dark brown to pale yellow in colour and available in thick slabs. Jaggery has a richer taste than refined sugar, almost like dark brown sugar. It is used to temper or enhance sweet as well as hot and sour dishes. It is usually added just before the dish is fully cooked.

Lemon juice. Bottled lemon juice is as good as fresh lemon juice and a lot cheaper, very useful to add acidity to food. Also see citric acid.

Mace (nutmeg husk). ★★ Mace has a sweet and warm flavour and is used in many sweet dishes. It is usually added towards the end of cooking. It is also sprinkled on top of deserts. You need only a small quantity.

Mustard seeds (black). A very commonly used item in all Asian dishes. Usually whole black mustard seeds are thrown into hot oil for seasoning before adding the rest of the spices. They immediately start popping up. Do not wait until the last one pops up, make sure they do not burn.

Nutmeg. ★★ See also mace. Nutmeg is a nut and used in small quantities in deserts by grating. Best to use a nutmeg grater for this purpose.

Poppy seeds. ★★ Used to give a rich flavour and thicken gravies and sauces.

Red chilli powder. Gives heat and colour. Comes in different strengths and shades of red. Usually very red coloured chilli powder is less hot.

Red chilli (dried) whole. Add a couple of lightly crushed whole chillies to the hot oil for cooking vegetable or meat dishes. Throw a couple into home-made soups while cooking. Whole chilli has a slightly different warm flavour than powdered chilli or green chilli. Sometimes the whole chilli is lightly fried in oil then pounded and added to dry chutneys. [Dry-roast sesame seeds, peanuts, desiccated coconut, and urid daal; add fried whole chillies and grind them together with a pinch of salt to make a spicy mix. Use it on its own or add to yogurt].

Red paprika or cayenne pepper. Gives an aromatic flavour but milder than using chilli.

Root ginger. See also ginger garlic paste. Very common ingredient for Chinese stir-fries, also for making delicately flavoured vegetables. [Add thinly sliced ginger to hot oil or butter and add small florets of broccoli , some black pepper and a pinch of salt, cook with lid on for three four minutes. Makes a crunchy lightly spiced side dish.]

Salt. Salt is available both as table salt, which is usually sea salt, and rock salt usually bought as crystals and used with a salt grinder. I prefer rock salt for cooking purposes. Always add salt last. Many vegetables contain natural salt and do not require too much salt. If you are making soup using stock cubes or ready-made stock, remember that the stock usually has salt in it, therefore taste the soup before adding any salt. Do not add salt to meats or pulses until they are almost cooked otherwise they will not cook properly.

Sesame seeds.★★ Used to add rich flavour and thickness to curries. Tahini paste is ready-made ground sesame seeds and very commonly used in far-eastern cookery.

Soy sauce. Comes as dark and light soy sauce. You can use just dark soy sauce for all your dishes. It is very useful for many Chinese dishes especially stir-fries though I use it for all kinds of dishes including soups and vegetables.

Tamarind paste/sauce. ★★ Tamarind is the pulp of the bean-like fruit of the tamarind tree. It is available in small jars. Deseeded tamarinds are also available but experimental cooks should stick to the paste as it is easier to use. The paste has a strong sour taste and is used to add acidity and flavour to curry dishes.

Tomato ketchup. I need not add any more here! You can use it in many ways. I also use it for adding to dips, marinades, and sometimes instead of tomato paste.

Tomato purée. Very useful to add to curries to add a sweet, sour flavour.

Turmeric. This is a yellow powder made from the root of the haladi plant. Although in the west it is known for its colour (which, by the way, is quite strong and the stains are difficult to remove), it has subtle flavour and also aroma. It is added to onion or vegetables or meat while it is cooking, **NOT** to the hot oil. Use in small quantities; too much will taste bitter.

A note about cooking onions

Although an onion is not a spice, it is used in many dishes for preparing the base with various spices. There are many ways to cook onion depending upon the type of dish.

Therefore I have chosen to include this note in the spices section because it seems to be the most appropriate place for it. Always add chopped onion to hot oil. Have sufficient hot oil before you add the onion, do not add more oil during the time the onion is cooking. Stir the onion a little to stop it from burning. When the onion changes its appearance from raw to glazed and translucent it is basically cooked; that is stage one. Further cooking makes the onion golden brown; that is stage two. If you cook it further it will turn brown, that is stage three, and if you cook it further still it will turn dark brown and caramelised, that is stage four. Different recipes require the onion to be cooked up to different stages. **It is important to note that you must not chop the onion for stage three and four, instead slice them thinly.** We will have a look at all of them.

Stage one: has a glazed appearance. This is used for most of the vegetable and other savoury dishes like semolina, couscous etc., where you do not want to create any gravy. At this stage it still has some onion flavour and crunchiness and, depending upon the type of onion, it will have some hotness also. Most white onions have more heat in them than red ones. Do not chop the onion too finely otherwise some of the onion might become too soft and watery. Roughly chopped is better suited for this stage. You can also chop it into larger chunks, but must ensure that it is properly cooked. Chop the onion into slightly larger chunks if you want to make a vegetable dish mainly out of onions (or shallots) with the addition of a few peas, sweetcorn or potatoes.

Stage two: the onion looks a light golden brown. It turns sweeter. This stage is more suitable when you want to create gravy or sauce for a curry or stew, or to make a spicy sauce to pour over some grilled or baked dish. For this you should chop the onion finely. Add little spices while it is cooking which makes the sauce spicy. You can always adjust the spices and add some more when the rest of the dish is cooking. If you are making a meat curry or lentil curry, add these to the onion when cooked. Brown and cook them and add any more spices if you want after tasting. When cooking diced lamb or pork it is also possible to brown the meat separately in oil, butter or ghee, set aside and then add to the cooked onion. This method gives meat a unique and rich flavour and is quite common in North Indian cuisine (they usually use ghee).

Stage three: the onion turns brown and has a bitter-sweet taste. Onion cooked this way is usually useful to mix with savoury rice dishes like biryani or for adding to fried dishes like sausages, chops etc. to give them an extra bit of flavour. **Do not chop the onion, slice it thinly.**

Stage four: the onion has a dark brown colour and a caramelised appearance. Any further cooking will burn the onion. This is typically used for mixing with and topping up biryani dishes and other savoury rice dishes. It gives the dish a smoky and bitter flavour typical of biryani dishes and is excellent for garnishing daals. **Do not chop the onion, slice it thinly.**

Smoking technique

This is another technique that is best included in this section. You have probably seen chefs using a smoke-producing machine to add a smoky flavour to some dishes. Using smoke to enhance flavour of certain dishes like biryani and savoury rice is an old method practised in the Indian continent for a few centuries. It is particularly suited for biryani dishes with meat. You do not need any machine to do this. I will show you how.

First prepare your rice dish, biryani for example. Set it aside in a pan with lid. A glass bowl with lid or a pan with glass lid is ideal because then you can observe the whole process. Have a little oil or ghee in a small dish and set it aside.

The next stage is best performed when you are about to serve the dish.

If your biryani or rice dish has become cool, you need to warm it up again before proceeding with smoking. If it is in a microwave compatible container like a glass bowl, warm it in the microwave otherwise you have to warm it on the hob and put it back into the serving dish. The bowl or dish must have a lid to keep the smoke trapped inside the container.

Have a small metal dish or small metal bowl ready at hand. Now take piece of charcoal (as used for a barbecue), it should be a about a couple of inches wide, and place it on a lit gas burner. Sorry for the people with an electric hob; it won't work for them this way. Wait until the charcoal starts burning and glowing like an ember.

Carefully pick up the charcoal with tongs and place it in the small metal plate. Then place the plate containing the charcoal on the top of the rice in the bowl with its burning side facing up, pour a tsp of the oil/ghee on the red-hot part of the charcoal, make sure it is now producing smoke and cover the bowl with a lid. Wait till the smoke dies down. Take the charcoal out and serve your dish immediately, for the smoky effect will fade away in the next half hour or so.

You can use the smoking technique for daals, some vegetables also. It gives a new kind of flavour to these dishes. In this case it is best to use a small bowl for the charcoal because it will float over the daal.

11

USEFUL HINTS

NOTE: You may find some of these hints also included other sections in context with the particular subject discussed. The list here is intended for a reference for general purposes.

Preparation

» Plan your dish ahead: take out the ingredients required and set them aside in the required quantities in separate containers near you. Decide the order in which you will add them during the cooking process.

» Parallel processing: you can do many things at the same time. For example chop the vegetables for soup or stew while your stock cube or stock pot is dissolving in warm water; or put away the used pots and pans while the food is simmering.

» Slicing garlic or ginger for stir-frying: there is no need to peel the skin. Slice them thinly in large slices and then shred them again by slicing through them. The amount of skin left is negligible.

Cooking vegetables

» Check the taste before adding salt to vegetables. Generally, leaf vegetables require very little salt.

» Do not cook green leafy vegetables with the lid on. They tend to change colour and become soggy. Leafy vegetables require very little cooking.

» You can use the tender stems of many leafy vegetables, they add more flavour to the dish. Chop them a little more finely than the rest of the vegetable.

» Cooking daals and pulses: always soak them in warm water for two to three hours till they swell and become softer. Do not add salt till the daal is nearly cooked. If you are using pulses in soups or stews which will be cooked slowly for a longer time, then there is no need to soak.

» Refreshing stale vegetables: if the vegetables have lost their fresh look soak them in cold water for an hour or so then drain and use.

» Always soak chunks of cabbage and sliced leeks in water before using. The reason is that these vegetables grow layer by layer and it is wise to ensure that there is no trapped dirt between the layers.

» Cooking mushrooms: if you want dry crispy mushrooms, use a wok. Add a large knob of butter to the hot wok, tip in the mushrooms (small button mushrooms are the best but other types will do as well). Sprinkle plenty of pepper and a pinch of salt. Do not stir, move the mushrooms by gently tossing around and leave without lid on for a minute or two. Mushrooms do not require any cooking as such. For extra rich flavour add a couple of tablespoons of cream and simmer of another minute or so.

» Preventing certain vegetables from becoming sticky as they cook: certain vegetables such as okra tend to

become sticky as they cook. This is because the protein
in the vegetables start forming a network of chains. To
break down these chains add some acidic ingredient
and stir it well. Keep stirring and the sticky gel will
disappear. The best ingredient to use is 'Amsul', available
in Asian shops in packets. It is the fruit of the kokum
tree. The botanical name is *gracinia indica*; it is sour
and brown in colour. You can also use tamarind paste
(also available from Asian shops) or try lemon juice or
vinegar. You only need a small amount.

Cooking meats

» Meat with a high proportion of connective tissues (such
as chicken legs or wings) should be cooked longer than
that with a lower proportion of connective tissues (such
as breasts).

» Steaks are cooked at high temperature for a shorter time,
therefore the meat will cook better if any connective
tissues are trimmed off before cooking.

» Always brown the outside of meat at a high temperature.
This helps to develop flavour because the large surface
protein molecules break down at high heat and the
amino acids combine with sugars to produce the
characteristic flavour. This is known as the Maillard
reaction.

» Use less spices when cooking meats with a fair amount
of bones in them than when cooking chunky pieces of
meat with very little bones (based on the weight). The
spices do not add any flavour to the bones.

Part II: The Art of Cooking

Making stocks, gravies, sauces and soups

» Add vegetables and onions to stock to improve the flavour.

» Sweat the vegetables and onions before adding to stock; this will produce jelly-like structures, improving the texture of the stock. The same is true in the case of gravies.

» If you want the stock or gravy a little darker, then brown the vegetables.

» If you want to, freeze the stock then concentrate it by boiling off excess water. Note that you may lose some of the flavour.

» To avoid the sauce or gravy going lumpy ensure that the starch granules in the flour do not stick together as you add water or other liquid. The way to do this is to disperse the granules, preventing them from coming together and forming lumps, either by mixing the flour in little cold water before adding to the sauce or by using oil or fat (such as butter) that coats the granules, preventing them from sticking together.

Storing food

» If your onion is too big, you can store the leftover onion in an airtight box in the fridge for a few days and use it later. Best to store a large piece rather than chopped onion.

» Garlic and ginger are best stored in covered pots with ventilation holes. They are available in shops or from mail order catalogues. They also keep well for a longer

116

time in thick cloth bags that stop light going through.

» Store onions and potatoes in light-proof bags. Purpose-made bags are available and they work well and are worth the money.

» Green chillies are quite expensive. Stored in the fridge, they become brown and soggy in three to four days. They will last a little longer if stored in a brown paper bag and then left in the fridge. However I have found a better way. I wrap the chillies in a small piece of newspaper and put them in a nylon bag with an open mesh (like a strainer). I have found such purpose-made bags in India. However you can improvise by using the small bags that are used to pack garlic bulbs. Chillies stored in this way will last up to three or four weeks.

» Storing coriander: the main reason that coriander does not keep for long without starting to rot is that it is usually sold wet and has some soil attached to its roots. This starts the natural process of deterioration. Coriander does not freeze well. The best way to store it is to make sure it is thoroughly dry. Do not wash it unless it is too soiled – in that case wash it, drain and thoroughly dry. Before storing spread the coriander thinly on a tray and check for any leaves that are turning brown or black, which should be discarded. Unless the stems are too long for your box they should be left on. Divide a large bunch into two or three manageable smaller bunches. Wrap each of them in newspaper (not tissues or plastic or grease proof paper which does not deal with any condensation that will be produced during storage). Now line a thick-walled plastic box with newspapers and place the wrapped up parcels inside and top them up with another sheet of newspaper before closing the lid. Try not to leave too much empty space in the box; if necessary, fill it with newspaper. The air contains moisture and it condenses when cool and makes things damp. Now wrap up the whole box with newspaper and place it in a plastic bag and place it on the middle or higher shelf in the fridge. The idea is to keep it cool but not near zero temperature. Inspect the coriander about every five days to check for any black leaves and moisture and if necessary repeat the procedure that you followed when packing it initially. The coriander will keep in quite good condition for up to three or four weeks depending upon the quality and condition of the coriander that you bought.

» Yogurt lasts for a longer time if the plastic container is stored upside down. Wrap the top tightly in aluminium kitchen foil and then in a cling film with a tight rubber band around it before storing. This is makes the pot airtight and gives fewer chances for bacteria to grow. This method should also work with other foods packed in a similar way.

» Lettuce and vegetables like cabbage or pak choi that contain a lot of water in their leaves last a lot longer in the fridge if they are wrapped in greaseproof paper.

Freezing food

» Chutneys made from coriander and chillies freeze well. It is easier to make chutney in a larger quantity. However one only needs a small amount at a time. The best way to freeze is to use an ice cube tray and freeze the chutney as cubes. Place the tray in a freezing plastic bag before placing in the freezer. When frozen you can use them as needed. It lasts for a very long time.

» Milk freezes well. Freeze on the day you buy. Do not use a glass container because the volume will increase as the milk freezes and break the container. Use the plastic bottles as supplied by the supermarkets. Frozen milk will keep for a long time but it is best to consume it within three months. Shake well after defrosting.

» Yogurt, like milk, freezes quite well. The problem is that the water in the yogurt tends to crystallise. When defrosted you get thick watery nodules suspended in watery buttermilk type liquid. Actually this makes quite a refreshing drink. Just add some black pepper and a pinch of salt and some chopped mint, a lovely drink on its own or with any savoury dish. However if you want to limit the crystallisation then stir the yogurt well before freezing. As an additional precaution you can add small amount of vodka <u>before</u> stirring which acts as an antifreeze. But do not overdo as it might hinder the freezing process!

» Bread freezes well. You can separate the slices into manageable numbers and pack them in freezer bags. Ensure that you have removed excess air by pressing around the bag before tying the top. This will keep condensation to the minimum.

» Defrosting milk: Leave the frozen milk in a cool place overnight. When most of the milk has defrosted, shake the bottle well to ensure that the milk residue and water is mixed together again.

» Defrosting bread: leave in a box without any wrapping till defrosted. If you need just a slice or two in hurry, use the toaster for a few seconds, not the microwave which makes it quite soft.

» Labelling storage boxes: wrap the storage box containing the items to be frozen in a cling film and then write on it with a permanent ink pen. This is an easier way as some plastic storage boxes are difficult to write on and also you can reuse the box for storing different item.

» If your storage box is larger than you need, wrap your food in a smaller plastic bag or cling film and put it in the box. You can then add other items to the same box; in addition this excludes extra air from coming into contact with the food in the bag.

Cleaning

» Tarnished pots and other items: brush on an acidic ingredient such as lemon, vinegar or tamarind paste and use a scouring pad. For really tarnished utensils or brass items with green verdigris you may require more than one attempt. Tamarind works best especially with brass, pewter etc. When using for any special or precious articles, always try on a small area, preferably one normally hidden from view, or take appropriate advice.

» Burnt pots and pans: Keep them dry and take the worst off by gently scraping away the burnt food. Make a thick paste of baking soda (sodium bicarbonate) in water. Cover the burnt area generously and leave for at least twelve hours. Then clean the dried paste off with a paper tissue and brush the pan with a hard brush with a little hot water (do not flood the pan). Then, using a scouring pad, try clearing any residues left. Sometimes you might have to repeat this process.

» The greasy frying pan or baking tray is easier to clean if you wipe off the grease using a tissue paper before it cools down. Wear gloves to protect your hands!

Miscellaneous

» If a recipe requires fresh grated coconut, you can instead use desiccated coconut. Mix the required quantity with enough cold milk to make it into a porridge-like consistency. Leave it in the fridge covered with cling film. Take out after 12 to 24 hours. Most of the milk will have been absorbed by the coconut. Drain any excess milk by lightly squeezing (do not squeeze dry). Leave in the fridge for another couple of hours if still too soggy, otherwise use it as it is.

» You can enhance the flavour of certain oily condiments such as whole black pepper, coriander seed, cumin, cloves etc. by dry roasting them in a frying pan for a couple of minutes and then pounding (rather than grinding). This makes the oil come out and enhances the flavour.

» There is an easier way to finely chop onions and vegetables like carrots, cucumber etc. Slice the vegetable such as an onion in circular disks about three millimetres thick and then chop them across into finer pieces. You get very similar result as the traditional way followed by chefs. Onion rings: You can take a few slices off the onion without peeling it.

» There is no reason why you should not try using Asian spices in your experimental western dishes. For example use coriander instead of parsley for fish and prawn dishes. It imparts much flavour and aroma and improves the dish. Sprinkle garam masala when grilling tomatoes (to eat with bacon or sausages or for adding to burgers). These spices work well with stews, grilled meats and fish also.

PART III: YOUR STAPLE INGREDIENTS AND HOW TO COOK THEM

A note about this section:

The ingredients included here are specially selected for their versatility and usefulness for experimental cooks. These ingredients are the basis of most of the dishes in all types of cuisines. If you experiment and learn how to use these ingredients as shown in this section, you can turn out dozens of dishes from each of these ingredients.

There is enough information in this section for you to get started. I have deliberately not given exact proportions of the various other ingredients. This is because I do not want you to get bogged down in the detail of producing one particular dish in a set manner. Instead, the idea is to explore the techniques and create your own dishes. There is sufficient information on various choices and combinations for you to try. So explore and learn something new. **Remember that you can use this information for producing main and side dishes from any cuisine.**

A note about food hygiene

It is important to wash raw ingredients such as meats and fresh vegetables properly in clean water. I have specifically used the word '**clean water**' because in some parts of the world the quality of water is not good, in which case you should use bottled or reliable filtered water. It is a good policy to soak the vegetables for twenty minutes or so before washing and the drain the water and wash them under a running tap. This not only cleans the vegetables but the soaking also freshens them. The meat and fish should be placed in a bowl in the sink and immersed in cold water and washed thoroughly by gently rubbing around. Then drain it and take to the chopping board for any cutting or trimming of fat. It is important to avoid splashing the liquid around, especially on to the worktop. If you do, spray the worktop with cleansing fluid and wipe it clean. The washing not only keeps the contamination at bay but washes away most of the stagnant blood which may contain toxic material. Always wash your hands after handling meat before touching other foods. Always clean the chopping board and keep the chopping board for meats separate from that used for other materials. Do not forget to clean the utensils used before putting them to any other use.

A note about relative proportions of the spices and other ingredients

(Also refer to Part II section 10 for descriptions of various individual bases for vegetables, curries, daals which can also be used for western dishes such as stews, goulash, pies etc.).

As stated above, I have not given the exact proportions of the ingredients required. This is deliberate. The whole idea behind the approach in this book is for you to experiment. However if you feel desperate to know the proportions for any particular recipe you can easily find that in cook books and on the internet. By experimenting you will learn how the various ingredients change the flavour and allow you to create your own particular version.

However, following is **a rough guide** of relative proportion of various spices used in most Asian dishes. You can experimentally use similar judgement if you are using any of these spices for other than Asian dishes. After using this guide a few times you can adjust the proportion to your taste.

Remember you do not necessarily need all the ingredients listed here for every recipe.

For meat curries and stews based on about 300g of meat (for about two servings):

Most of the meat recipes require cooking an onion before adding marinated meat

For the marinade
Two to three tsps of garlic and ginger paste (garlic 60%: root ginger 40% or if you prefer 50% each)

2 tsps of coriander powder.

1 tsp of cumin powder. (The strength of this powder varies: use less if it is very strong).

2–3 tsps of hot red chilli powder (the strength varies from brand to brand).

½–1 tsp of turmeric powder (do not overdo this unless you are sure, it can make food taste bitter if overdone).

1–1½ tbsp garam masala (there are many available, the taste and strength may vary, once you are happy with one brand, stick with it for a while. The garam masala generally contains cumin and coriander powder so adjust the proportion of these ingredients if using garam masala).

Optional yogurt – enough to cover the meat – or lemon juice.

For frying meat
One medium onion: about 100g (refer to notes on chopping onion in section 6).

Optional: pinch (less than half a teaspoon) of asafoetida (this is a very strong spice, and added to hot oil just before the onion or main ingredient is added. Do not let it burn).

For vegetable and daal dishes based on two cups of prepared vegetables (two servings):

The proportion of ingredients is the same except you will need to scale down the amount depending upon the volume/weight of the vegetables.

Again the list below is for relative proportions only, not all the ingredients are required in the same recipe.

One to two teaspoons of mustard seeds (to be added to hot

oil; do not let them burn).

Instead of ginger and garlic paste use three or four cloves of garlic. Ginger is normally not used.

About eight curry leaves. Added to hot oil, it gives a pungent flavour and a particular aroma found in South Indian dishes.

Fenugreek seeds: two or three maximum (excess will turn the dish bitter).

Any of the above spices are added to the hot oil before adding and cooking vegetables.

If using onion, add chopped onion after the spices, cook it and then add the vegetables.

Other ingredients used with any dishes: Meat, vegetables or savoury daals etc.

Use two to three teaspoons of cumin seeds added to hot ghee or oil for dry cooking potato cubes; this method does not require any other spice apart from salt and pepper (or chilli). Not suitable for curries.

Cinnamon and clove powder mixture, about one teaspoon, adds distinctive aroma and flavour.

Fenugreek leaves (dry or fresh), about ten. This adds a slightly bitter taste to bland vegetables and daals.

Mango powder, about half a teaspoon, gives a sour taste to food.

When cooking meats or pulses add salt towards the end.

There is more information on how to make the base for curries and vegetables in Section 10. Again, all the ingredients listed here are not always required.

12

RICE

Rice is one of the most versatile main ingredient for many types of dishes from all over the world. In India it is the staple food in many regions and an essential accompaniment to curry dishes. It is also eaten on its own like in biryani and savoury rice dishes. Egg fried rice is one of the most popular dishes from Chinese cuisine. Nowadays rice has also gained popularity in the western world.

Rice is one of the ingredients that experimental cooks should learn to cook properly as this will open doors to many types of dishes that you can experiment with and enjoy. You will find that cooking perfect rice is not that difficult if you follow my few simple instructions.

It is essential to know a bit about types of rice and how to choose it before trying to cook the rice as there are many types, and each is suited for a particular use.

Buying and storing rice

As stated above, there are many different types of rice suitable for different uses such as for rice dishes as found in Eastern and Indian cuisine, paella rice, rice for puddings etc. We are concerned here only with rice for Eastern and Indian dishes. The two main varieties you will come across here are basmati rice and Thai jasmine rice. I will briefly mention the cooking of Thai rice later. We will mostly concentrate on the basmati rice here.

Basmati rice

There are many dozens of varieties of cooking rice available in the Indian continent. The grains of each one have a different appearance and when cooked result in rice of different flavour and texture. Basmati is one of these types. It is grown in many parts of India and Pakistan, and widely exported from the Indian subcontinent.

The quality of basmati rice varies according to the region where it is grown and also the age of the rice. Newly harvested rice contains more moisture in the grain and is cheaper. Always look for rice which is at least two to three years old and matured. The colour should be off white to slightly ivory, not pure white (which the new rice is). The grains should be thin (not stubby), long and free from fluff or dust. The rice is usually packed in transparent bags and you can check this before buying. There are some good cheaper brands available but if you are new to rice go for the well-known brands.

Store the rice in a dry place in sealed bags or air-tight jars. Rice stored properly will last many months.

Cooking techniques

You probably have seen many techniques for cooking rice on TV or have come across them in books. They all work to an extent depending upon how you follow the whole process and the particular basmati rice. I will show you how to cook practically any rice (except Thai which I will deal with later) perfectly.

The process is explained through several steps to make it easy to follow. The advantage of my method over others is that it will work with almost any type of rice (but not puddings or paella rice) and, what is more, you can cook the rice according to your particular choice. Some prefer the rice almost dry and every grain separate, some a little moist and so on. You can do this by adjusting the amount of water and method of soaking.

The actual cooking process of rice takes less than 20 minutes. For the best enjoyment rice should be eaten while it is hot although you can store and reheat it again. There are many dishes where you use pre-cooked rice. I am aware of some western cooks' opinion about not reheating the rice and I will come to that later.

Cooking rice involves the following steps

Step 1: Take out the required amount of rice (about 70g per serving). Using a measuring jug note the volume of rice. The reason for this is that we will use this measure to decide how much water we will need to cook the rice.

Step 2: Put the rice into a large bowl and wash it under the cold tap while rubbing it thoroughly with your fingers. You will find that the water turns whitish and cloudy as you rub. Keep emptying the bowl and repeating the process at least four times by which time the water will be fairly clean.

Cleaning this way helps the rice grains to separate when cooked. Drain the water.

Step 3: Measure out fairly hot water which should be twice the volume of rice.

Step 4: Add the water to the bowl of rice and let it soak for at least one hour.

Step 5: Heat a cooking pot sufficiently large to accommodate about two-and-a-half to three times the volume of rice. Add about two to three teaspoons of margarine, ghee, or butter (not oil). Allow the fat to melt but not overheat.

Step 6: Spoon out the rice leaving as much water in the bowl as possible. Do not throw the water away, you will be using it. Add the rice to the pot and stir it so as to coat all the grains with the melting fat.

Step 7: Immediately add the water you left behind in the bowl and stir the rice so as to ensure that it is not sticking to the pan. Do not cover the pot at this stage; if you do, the water will boil over the edge of the pot and you will lose a lot of it. Add one teaspoon of salt, turn the heat to medium and wait till it starts boiling.

Step 8: Stand by the cooker. In a few minutes the water will start going down and the mixture will start bubbling. Watch till only small layer of water is left on the surface and large crater-like holes will appear in the rice.

Step 9: Reduce heat, you are only a few minutes away from finishing the rice. Cover the pot for a couple of minutes, you will see steam coming out from under the cover. Carefully lift the cover and pick up a small amount of rice and test it by crushing between your fingers. You should feel no more than a tiny grain if the rice is almost cooked. If it is go to step 11, if not go to step 10.

Step 10: If the rice feels grainy and there is not much water left, add a small amount (about two to three tablespoons) of water according to the dryness of the rice being cooked. Keep the pot covered, ensure that steam is coming from under the cover which is an indication that the water has not dried, in which case rice will burn.

Step 11: If the rice has almost cooked, spray a small amount of water on the top. It helps to generate more steam without making it soggy and helps the final cooking. This is a method I have developed myself. I use a small water spraying bottle available as an accessory in art shops. (Used for spraying over dried paint). You can sprinkle some water instead. Put the lid on, watch the steam coming out for a minute and turn the heat off. Leave the lid on for two three minutes. The rice should be ready to serve.

To change the texture

Add more water to make it moist. It could be added either at the beginning or halfway through or during stage 8. You cannot make it moist after it is cooked. If the rice is slightly moister than you require then cover it and leave it in the fridge overnight. You will find the rice is drier than what you left.

Key points about rice

» Always buy good quality basmati rice at least two to three years old.

» Look for long, thin yellowish coloured clean grains without fluff.

» Always wash the rice thoroughly and always soak it.

» The amount of water required for cooking depends upon the age of the rice and how long you have soaked it. New rice will require less water.

» Use sufficiently large a pot for the rice to swell and cook properly.

» Experiment with any rice you have not previously used by using no more than twice the volume of water, then adjust accordingly.

» Always add some fat like margarine before adding rice to the pan.

» Always add some salt. Salt gives the rice flavour.

» The final stage of cooking with the lid on is important for perfect cooking of the rice.

» Thai rice is a bit sticky and requires a different proportion of water. Follow the instructions on the packet.

Do you know that you do not need curry to enjoy rice?

In the West rice is usually associated with curry but you do not necessarily need curry to enjoy rice. In India for example, people sometimes have rice on its own with yogurt or milk and it is delicious! The rice must be freshly cooked and served immediately for this to work properly. If eating with milk always use cold milk straight from the refrigerator. Make a well in the rice in your plate, add enough milk so that it just starts running out at the sides. Add some salt (you need a salty taste). If eating with yogurt you can use cold rice if you prefer. Here add just a few tablespoons of yogurt and mix it. You can use any type of yogurt according to your preference, most people like slightly sour yogurt.

For added flavour when eating with milk or yogurt, have some chutney, raita, pickle or any vegetable dish as a side dish.

Rice dishes for the experimental cook

Plain rice with variations

Rice is very versatile. Once you can cook plain rice you can make huge number of dishes. This is an excellent field for the experimental cook. Many of the variations of rice dishes can be eaten on their own without any other side dish. You can have some chutney or raita or some sort of relish with it if you wish.

Savoury rice

Rice can be made savoury either during the process of initial cooking or afterwards. For making the rice savoury all you need is to use one of the base seasonings described in Section 10 and add the soaked rice to it and cook. The simplest seasoning is just mustard seeds in hot oil, add the rice then pinch of turmeric, some red chilli powder and some unroasted peanuts (optional).

Meat biryani

Please refer to Section 23: Vegetables, Daals and Main Dishes

Vegetable biryani

Cook a mixture of vegetables such as peas, sweetcorn, carrots and sweet peppers with some onion using one of the seasoning bases described in Section 10. Set aside.

Fry some sliced onion so that it is almost caramelised. Set aside.

Cook rice. Rice should be cooked so that it is fluffy and the grains do not stick to each other. For this you need to watch the water as described above in 'Cooking rice'. Let the rice cool.

In a large microwaveable bowl put layers of rice separated by a layer of vegetables, and alternate layers of the fried onion. Microwave for about three minutes just before serving.

If you like, use the smoking technique (explained at the end of Section 10) to give the biryani its authentic smoky flavour. Serve with raita or chutney.

Sweet rice

Sweet rice is quite popular in India. Cook the rice as usual except use ghee and add some cloves and cardamoms to the ghee before adding the rice. The rice should be cooked to be nice and fluffy, so watch the water. Let the rice cool. Make a mixture of fresh grated coconut (or desiccated coconut soaked overnight in milk), sultanas, almond flakes and sugar. Taste the mixture; it should be fairly sweet because we will be adding rice to it. Add the cooked rice to the mixture and mix thoroughly. Sprinkle a dash of water and warm in a microwave in a covered bowl till it is nice and steaming hot. Sprinkle a few strands of saffron on the top (optional). Serve immediately.

Rice pudding

For rice pudding you need pudding rice. Follow the instructions on the packet. Basically all you need to do is add about 600 to 700ml of milk to about 100g of pudding rice, add about 50g of sugar, sprinkle some grated nutmeg and bake at low temperature (about 150°C) in the oven for a couple of hours in a greased baking dish.

About reusing cooked rice:

Like most Asians, I have been reusing cooked rice without encountering any problems. I believe properly washed, soaked and cooked rice can be perfectly well reused within a couple of days if stored properly in the fridge. However, it is up to you whether you should reuse the cooked rice or not. In fact cooked rice is ideal for making delicious savoury fried rice. (Season with mustard seeds, garlic, onion and green chillies and garnish with fresh chopped coriander). Rice for biryani is traditionally cooked in advance and cooled before using in the biryani dish. Chinese fried rice is made from pre-cooked rice.

13

POTATOES

In Western cuisine potato is commonly used as an accompaniment to meat or fish in the form of chips, boiled or baked potato. It is also used as topping for some pies like shepherd's pie or fish pie. Fish and chips is of course one of the top dishes in the UK. Potato is also hugely popular on the Indian continent and there are literally hundreds of side dishes and snacks made using the potato.

For the experimental cook potato is one of the easiest staple ingredient to cook. Most experimental cooks would have some sort of experience of cooking potatoes like boiled potato or jacket potato. We will look at the various ways of cooking potato and some simple but delicious dishes you can have a go at.

Various ways of cooking potato

Boiling

You can boil them with the skin on or peeled. Always add a little salt to the water. You can use the hob or microwave. If you are boiling for making mash then peel them and cut into halves or quarters: that way it is easier to mash.

Baking and roasting

If you are roasting meat or other vegetable then roast them together at the same time. Peel the potatoes and drizzle some olive oil and bake them in the tray. You can also bake them in a foil.

Grilling

Cut the potatoes into wedges, drizzle some oil over them, sprinkle any spices or salt, pepper or chilli flakes and grill them in a thick bottomed grill pan with little oil.

Cooking in pan

This is really an excellent area to experiment and create your own recipes. You can make a variety of potato vegetables on their own or mixed with any other vegetables either dry, moist or as curries. Use one of the Basic Spice Mixtures (see Section 10). Experiment with the size and shape of the way you chop the potatoes; you will find you will change the texture and the taste. You can try adding cooked or semi cooked potatoes to other vegetables or curries especially meat or shellfish curries and add some hot seasoning on the top.

You will find a couple of potato recipes in Section 23.

Here is sample of interesting dishes that you might like to try

Jacket potato

Bake the potato in a microwave, slice it open and top up with fillings such as mayonnaise, ketchup, lettuce, cheese, coleslaw etc.

Mashed potato

Boil potatoes, mash them, add butter and salt while mashing. Soften it with a dash of milk. You can use this basic mash as a side dish with any meat or sausages etc. Or make shepherd's pie using pre-cooked mince, or mix it with spices and chilli and make small flat cakes using the shallow frying method. You need to brush the cakes with beaten eggs to stabilize the cake and stop it from crumbling.

Potato wedges

See grilling above.

Potato chips

You can make your own chips freshly. Slice the potatoes into chips the size you want, drizzle oil and sprinkle any spices or salt and pepper and bake them till brown, no need to fry.

Grated savoury potato

Refer to the recipe in Section 22.

Potato salad

Boil potatoes. Baby potatoes are the best for this recipe. Let them cool and cut into small pieces. Mix them with mayonnaise, gherkins, capers, salt and pepper with a dash of lemon juice and serve with hard boiled eggs.

14

PASTA AND NOODLES

Pasta is another one of those ingredients that is easy to cook and very useful for experimental cooks.

Types of Pasta

There are many dozens of types of pasta. Here are a few that most of you have probably come across.

» Calamarata: Wide, ring shaped pasta.

» Fusilli: Long, thick, corkscrew-shaped pasta, can be either hollow or solid.

» Lasagne: Wide, thin sheets usually used like multi-layered sandwich of meat and baked.

» Linguine: This pasta is elliptical shaped rather than flat, and about 4mm wide.

» Macaroni: Hollow tubes, can be straight or curved, usually baked in cheese sauce.

» Pappardelle: Thick flat ribbons.

» Spaghetti: The well-known pasta used in spaghetti Bolognese.

» Tagliatelle: Pasta with narrower ribbons than pappardelle.

Noodles are a type of pasta that requires very little cooking and are favourite ingredients in Chinese dishes such as stir-fry, Chow Mein and many other dishes.

Cooking pasta

Some pasta needs baking in the oven. Pasta like spaghetti require boiling. Cooking instructions are always on the pack. See spaghetti Bolognese recipe in section 23.

Cooking noodles

Noodles require virtually no cooking. Some require pouring boiling water over and leaving for a few minutes, some require boiling. Follow the instructions on the pack.

Ideas for some dishes to experiment with

Spaghetti bolognese
See recipe in Part IV.

Macaroni
Macaroni is ideal for the experimental cook. It is easy to make, substantial and involves two different processes; making white sauce and baking.

You will need about 200g of macaroni, 20g plain flour, 30 to 40g butter and 500 to 550ml of milk, 250g of farmhouse or mature Cheddar and some Parmesan cheese for the topping.

To make the sauce, melt the butter in a saucepan, add the flour and cook for a few minutes, then add the milk a little at a time and cook, stirring frequently, until the sauce thickens and becomes smooth. This will take about 15 minutes; do not let it burn. Then add most of the Cheddar into the sauce and stir it to dissolve. Set side.

Preheat your oven to 200°C, gas mark 6. While that is happening boil the macaroni in a saucepan for about 8 to 10 minutes or as per instructions on the packet. Drain. Add the sauce to the macaroni and mix it well. Transfer to an ovenproof baking dish and bake it till the macaroni is brown. All you are doing is browning the macaroni because everything is already cooked. Top it with some Cheddar or Parmesan and serve hot.

Tagliatelle

These are flat ribbons about between 6 to 10mm wide and are sold curled in nests or straight. They can be green in colour in which case they are flavoured with spinach.

Egg noodles and rice noodles

These noodles come in thick and thin varieties. They are quite easy to cook. They usually require leaving in very hot boiled water for five to six minutes or boiling in water. The instructions are always on the pack. Both are ideal for adding to stir-fry dishes. Egg noodles usually require a bit of cooking with the stir-fry. Rice noodles, being more delicate, need adding just towards the end of the stir-fry. Rice noodles can also be added to soups. Both types are excellent for experimental cooks to try.

15

COUSCOUS

Couscous is a kind of hard wheat semolina which has been ground then moistened and rolled into smaller grains. You can serve couscous with all kinds of meats and vegetable dishes instead of potatoes or rice. The variety available in UK in packets is pre-cooked and requires just the addition of boiling water. The instructions are always on the pack.

Other similar products made from wheat are cracked wheat, also called bulgur wheat, and semolina, which is coarsely ground wheat. This section contains ideas on how to cook and serve couscous. There is some information on dishes made from semolina in Section 10 and in Section 22.

Cooking couscous

Use the instant variety of couscous. It only needs the addition of boiling water. According to the instructions found on most packets, you need to add about 1¼ times the weight of boiling water. So if you have about 50g of couscous you need to add about 62g (62 ml) of boiling water, stir and leave for about 10 minutes.

Another easier way to cook couscous is to measure out the required amount of couscous in large bowl suitable for microwaving, (couscous will increase in volume about three times). Add stock (for better flavour) rather than water (warm or room temperature). The level of the liquid should just reach to the top of the grains; no more. Mix the whole thoroughly so that there are no dry grains left. You may need to add a little more water if you find that the grains are still not quite soaked. Leave for about 10 minutes. Add a couple of tablespoons of butter and any salt to taste (if required), mix it, cover the bowl and microwave for a couple of minutes on a medium setting.

You can increase the flavour of the cooked couscous by seasoning with spices, onion, red pepper etc. Couscous is a great alternative to rice, mashed potatoes and even chips. You can serve all types of meats and vegetables with couscous. Couscous can be frozen and reheated. It is a great dish for the experimental cook.

16

BREADS

Making bread is not difficult but requires considerable practice. Mixing various ingredients, the amount of water, kneading and proving needs to be just right otherwise you get lumpy stone-like bread or soggy bread. The bread should be spongy and, when gently pressed, should spring back. I think the experimental cook should instead try simple flat breads which are described in this section.

If you are adventurous and wish to bake bread then look for the many recipes available in cookery books or on the internet.

Paratha

INGREDIENTS

❖ 1½–2 cups (350–450 ml) of wholemeal flour (Atta)

❖ 2 tbsp ghee

❖ ½ tsp salt (or to taste as required)

❖ Water

❖ Oil for frying and for the flour.

METHOD

Mix the dry ingredients in a bowl. Add a tablespoon of oil to the flour and mix. Add a little water at a time and fork it in to make it into a soft dough. Make the dough into a ball shape and transfer it to a board sprinkled with some flour (so as not to stick to its surface).

Using your hands, make the ball into sausage shape about 1½ inches in diameter. Cut it into pieces about 2½ inches long.

Take one piece on the floured board and, using a rolling pin, roll into a circle about 4 inches in diameter. Apply some ghee to one side, sprinkle a little flour (helps to reduce the friction between layers) and fold it in half. Again apply some ghee, sprinkle flour and fold in half again.

Now gently roll it into a ball (do not press too tight) and roll it into a circle about ⅛ inch thick. Heat a frying pan on medium heat add some oil or ghee and transfer the paratha on it, put the lid on for a minute. Take the lid off and check if one side is cooked, then turn it over and repeat for the other side.

THALEE-PEETH: (literally means 'bread made on a plate')

This is a much easier version of the above. You mix the wholemeal flour and oil and salt as above and make about 2½ inch diameter balls. Using your hands flatten them into circular shapes about ¼ inch thick (thicker than the paratha above). Smear some ghee on one surface and transfer to a pan with a just a dash of oil. Cook both sides in the same way as the paratha, with the lid on. This type of flat bread will become a bit hard if stored, so it is best eaten on the same day.

17

MEAT, POULTRY, FISH AND SHELLFISH

I have not included too much information about cooking meat in this section because the essential information is covered in the recipe section and also in the reference section under the chemistry of cooking.

Meat is available from different animals and in different formats (processed and unprocessed). These are sold as pork, beef and lamb chops, steaks and joints, bacon, sausages and cooked meats. The cooking techniques are different for different types of meat.

As far as fresh and processed meats are concerned I think grilling and shallow frying are the simplest methods for experimental cooks. For this method of cooking, chops and steaks are the most suitable. Sausages and gammon steaks can be cooked either in the pan or in the oven.

Cooking meat as curry is covered in Part IV: Section 23, Main Meals.

Chicken is perhaps the easiest and quickest meat to cook. You can make curry in the same way as meat curry or cook it in the oven in foil or in a roasting bag, which is perhaps the easiest way for new cooks.

Fish is quite easy and quick to cook. The best way for

experimental cooks is to pan fry with very little spices or just mustard, pepper and salt or bake it in foil. The important thing is not to overcook the fish because it will become chewy.

Prawns are the easiest type of shellfish for experimental cooks. They are ideal for curries and stir-fry dishes. You can also use them to make a dry cooked side dish or to make rice biryani. Cooked prawns can be used in prawn cocktails, or added to a stir-fry towards the end. Uncooked prawns may require shelling and a bit of cleaning before cooking but these also cook very quickly. You will need to cook them with a little onion, garlic and ginger and some chilli powder.

Morphing

All types of leftover meats are very suitable for morphing. For example:

Leftover gammon and pineapple dish: slice into small strips and use it in stir-fry.

Leftover lamb chops: cut into smaller pieces, cook a little onion with any curry seasoning described in Section 10, add the pieces of chop and a little water, simmer gently for a few minutes, taste and add any additional spice or chilli flakes. You've got delicious meat curry!

Leftover mince: use for shepherd's pie, with spaghetti or any pasta, add to home-made soup while cooking. Use it for sandwiches.

Adding vegetables

You can add vegetables like spinach, sweetcorn, beans, all types of marrows, bhindi, potatoes etc. to most meat dishes including shellfish dishes, especially curries. Not only do they improve the flavour but also it is healthier and the meat goes much further this way.

18

PULSES AND DAALS

Lentils or pulses are the fruit or dry seed of plants that belong to the family of plants called Legume. Other edible seeds that belong to this family are peas and beans.

Daal is the processed variety of the whole pulse where the seed is split into two halves. Some daals have their outer layer removed and some are intact or have the husk partially removed. For example the moong daal comes as green moong daal with the outer layer intact and also as yellow moong daal with the outer layer removed. The two varieties have slightly different flavours.

Some of the fattish variety of pulses are also known as lentils; for example red lentils. Their split variety is also usually called lentils.

Note regarding the spelling of daal: in this book I have spelt 'daal' as per its phonetic spelling. Very often it is spelt with only one 'a' as 'dal'.

Daals are used to make curries (called cooked daal rather than curry); they can be added to soups, cooked with rice to make savoury rice, roasted and pounded with chilli and other spices to make into delicious South Indian type dips, fried and added to rice flakes to turn into Chewada (sometimes called 'Bombay Mix': a term I do not approve).

Whole pulses are actually seeds, so they are ideal for sprouting, a technique rarely described in cookery books. This is an open field for experimental cooks and worth trying as described in Section 21.

From the point of view of the experimental cook, many of the pulses and daals are ideal material. They are very easy to cook and versatile as we shall see in this section. Although there are many varieties of pulses and daals I would advise to concentrate on just the following:

Pulses: Whole green moong.

Daals: Green moong daal, yellow moong daal, red lentils.

Cooking daals and lentils

Always thoroughly wash them until the water runs clear. Soak them in warm water till they swell and become a bit soft. This might take from ½ to 1½ hours depending upon the variety.

For making soup

If you are making home-made soup then just wash the daal or lentils and add to the onion while cooking other vegetables. Then simmer and cook or use a slow cooker.

If your soup is already simmering in a pot or slow cooker then simply soak the daal or lentils till they are soft and add to the soup for extra flavour and body.

For making spicy daal

Wash and soak the daal or lentils. Chop some onion and cook with any spice base as described in Section 10, add the daal or lentils and cook. When cooking daal this way always add a pinch of asafoetida; you will find that this makes a lot of difference to the final taste. Red lentils are fine with or without asafoetida. If you do not have it then use cumin seeds and sliced root ginger in the seasoning base.

Cooking pulses

This is exactly the same as cooking daal, except that you will need to soak them for a few hours before they will swell on account of the outer skin. They will also need longer to cook. Use onion, ginger and garlic paste, garam or any other masala, chilli powder, turmeric powder etc. similar to any other curry recipe.

SPROUTING PULSES FOR MAKING CURRIES OR SALADS – *see also Section 21*

Wash and soak the pulses till they swell up. Drain most of the water leaving a little lying at the bottom of the pot. Moisten a thick cloth like a dish cloth and transfer the pulses into it. Tie up the cloth tightly with the pulses in it into a sort of a bundle which at this point will be dripping with water.

Transfer the bundle to a pot just large enough to hold the bundle. Cover the pot with an additional cloth to stop the loss of moisture. Leave this pot in a cool place out of direct sunlight for two to four days till the pulses sprout. You will need to open the bundle each day once or twice to check and moisten it. Do not let it dry out.

Once the pulses have sprouted, wash them gently in water at room temperature and transfer back into the bundle for ½ to 1 day. You will find that the sprouted shoots have grown about ½ to 1 cm. They are ready to be used. (Sprouting produces sugar and thus improves flavour).

The sprouted pulses can be added to salads. If you have enough you can make delicious curry. Use type 4 base (with asafoetida) and finely chopped onion. Add cinnamon and clove powder, mixed in at the end for an extra kick and flavour. Sprouted pulses cook very quickly, **do not overcook.**

19

SOUPS

Making your own soups at home is quite easy. One of the advantage of making soups is that you can use up any leftover items from your salad tray such as celery, leaks, carrots etc. You can also use other root vegetables like potatoes, sweet potatoes, turnips and so on.

The basics of making home-made soup is straightforward. All you need is vegetables and stock. For the stock you can either use stock granules or best of all use small stockpots available from the supermarkets as vegetable, chicken or beef stockpots. They are quite handy and one pot makes a pint of stock.

Alternatively stock can be made from bony carcass leftovers. To make chicken stock from chicken bones, place the chicken carcass, garlic, vegetables, herbs and peppercorns in a large, deep-bottomed pot. Add enough cold water and bring to the boil, skim the floating greasy layer on the surface as it rises. Then simmer the liquid on a low heat for three to four hours, skimming as required. When reasonably thick liquid is left pass the stock through a fine sieve.

TO MAKE VEGETABLE SOUP: (Using stockpot)

First get the stock going. Add the contents of the stockpot and let it dissolve.

Clean and cut the vegetables into about ½ inch pieces. If using carrots I like to chop them in crouton size pieces because they add good body when cooked. But you can cut the vegetables as you want. Usually celery and leeks make a good combination. You need a large bowlful of the vegetables (at least about ½ a litre in volume).

Roughly chop an onion. Slice a few cloves of garlic and a small piece of root ginger (less than ¼ inch).

Heat about a tablespoon of oil in a pan, add the garlic and ginger. If you want the soup to be on the spicy hot side then you can add one whole dried red chilli otherwise you can add black pepper later. Add the chopped onion and cook for a couple of minutes to soften it a little. Add the chopped vegetables and cook by gently stirring for three minutes or so. Add ½ a cup of water and simmer for a couple of minutes. Add the dissolved stock and stir to ensure the vegetables are not sticking to the bottom of the pan. (NOTE: if you are using the slow cooker from this point onwards follow the method as described below, otherwise continue). Cover and simmer for two to three hours on **LOW** heat. Check the water from time to time and add more as required. Do not add salt unless you taste first as the stock normally is salty. Adjust taste to requirement. The soup can be frozen and reheated.

Cooking with a slow cooker

I usually use the slow cooker instead of simmering on the hob. It requires less attention and the taste is a lot better. For this, start the process just as above. Then instead of simmering the stock in the pan, transfer the mixture to the slow cooker and cook according to the instructions for your cooker. (I use the auto setting on my cooker which switches between low and high). Cook for four to five hours. The advantage of the slow cooker method is you can add soft items such as cooked meats or soaked daals etc. later in the cooking so as they do not overcook. Slow-cooked soups made using meats are especially tasty: more so than the hob-cooked ones.

Making meat based soups

The process is exactly same as above except first you will need to cook the meat as you do for curry. The meat needs to be reasonably done before adding any vegetables and stock. A slow cooker is best suited for meat-based soups.

Ready to use soups

You can always use soup packets. There is a large variety of them available. The advantage here is it requires no preparation and you can still improve them by adding items like steamed spinach, rice noodles, grated cheese, croutons etc.

Accompaniments with soup

You can serve soup with toast, garlic bread, crumpets, savoury biscuits or a sandwich. I like a thick slice of brown bread toast with garlic paste rubbed on it.

20

VEGETABLES

Cooking vegetables is perhaps one of the most interesting, important and rewarding things to learn for the experimental cook, for several reasons. In western cuisine vegetables are generally treated as a 'side dish' usually made from potatoes, cabbage or broccoli or perhaps courgettes or Brussels sprouts, and cooked in a standard traditional way. However in Asian cuisine vegetables have an important place and there are many dozens of vegetables cooked in a variety of ways: some dry, some moist, some almost like curry. In Asian cuisine the vegetables are also cooked with pulses, daals, meats etc. So now you can get an idea why experimenting with vegetables will open many doors for you.

Types of vegetables

There are the following types of vegetables that are worth experiment with

Greens: like spinach, kale, broccoli, cauliflower, pak choi

Marrow type vegetables: like courgettes, marrow, pumpkins

Root vegetables: like carrots, potatoes, sweet potatoes, onions.

Beans: various types of beans and peas

Others: tomatoes, aubergine (brinjal), bhindi (okra), mushrooms, sweetcorn etc.

Cooking vegetables

Many delicate vegetables like leafy vegetables, courgettes, pak choi etc. can be simply cooked with only garlic and chilli (or black pepper). Chop the leafy vegetables roughly (courgettes and other marrow like vegetables should be chopped into small cubes). Add plenty of sliced garlic cloves to hot oil and when lightly pink add a couple of whole dried red chillies, or green if you prefer, add the vegetables to it and cook on medium heat for a few minutes. You will know when they are just cooked when the volume of the vegetables reduces or the colour changes. Do not put the lid on if cooking leafy vegetables, otherwise do put the lid on. Do not overcook. Cooking vegetables this way should not take more than 5 to 6 minutes, less if you prefer a crunchy texture. When adding garlic to the hot oil it is important that you do not let it burn. The trick is ensure that the oil is very hot, add garlic cloves and chillies and in a few seconds turn off the heat, watch the garlic changing colour, then put the heat back on and add the vegetables. Add salt after cooking if required.

Fresh cabbage, if finely shredded, can be eaten with just a little steaming. Refer to the recipes in section 23 for a simple, quick and delicious sambharo recipe. I prefer to use tender, pointed cabbage if available.

Mushrooms and courgettes require virtually no cooking. Refer to the recipe section for good ideas.

Marrows can be stuffed with a variety of fillings and shallow fried or steamed.

Beans, such as French beans, can be cooked quickly in a frying pan in some hot oil with cloves of garlic, a little ginger, pepper and salt and a dash of water to generate steam; then covered for two or three minutes.

These are just a few ideas for you to play with and try. There are several more ideas in the recipe sections in Part IV.

21

SPROUTING

Sprouting is a very much overlooked area in cookery books, yet it is simple and has many applications. I would recommend that you invest in a sprouting jar. It is basically a glass jam-jar with a lid that has perforations like a sieve. Usually the lid has a built in collar that allows the jar to be placed at a tilt to allow the water to seep out. The sprouting instructions are provided with the jar.

There are various types of sprouting seeds available in small or large packets to buy online or in specialist health shops. All you need to get started is put a small amount of seeds into the jar. (The volume grows four to five times after the seeds have fully sprouted.) Then wash out the seeds in the jar a couple of times with cold water and refill the jar and lay on its side in a dish to collect the seeping water which you empty from time to time.

Repeat the washing out and refilling with water every day; twice a day. You will see the seeds sprouting in a couple of days. The shoots keep growing. You can harvest the sprouted seeds as required in small quantities.

The sprouted seeds can be used with salads, soups, in stir-fry, in sandwiches and in a number of other ways.

Some seeds, like fenugreek, can sprout just by keeping moist in a shallow plate. These add quite an interesting bitter taste to salads.

PART IV: THE ART OF EXPERIMENTING

AND SOME DISHES FOR YOU TO TRY

If you have followed this book then you have come a long way from where you started. You have learned to look at your kitchen as a laboratory where you experiment with various processes using various ingredients to create some interesting food that you can enjoy.

You now have some knowledge of how the various chemicals in your ingredients react with each other and produce different textures, tastes and aromas. If you have made any mistakes in following the simple ideas in this book, or perhaps some other recipes, you are beginning to understand what might have gone wrong and maybe how to recover from it.

This part of the book takes you a step further, out of your comfort zone so to speak. There are many recipes in this section. I would rather call them sort of exercises. These are basic ideas in the form of templates. The ingredients listed for each recipe are approximate and you can vary the quantity or change any ingredients as you wish. As far the processes for each recipe are concerned, try them as I have suggested and then try to change them according to your inspiration.

169

You will find that the recipes and ideas in this book in general and in this section in particular relate to a variety of cuisines; in fact I would say they go across the cuisine barrier. I feel that experimental cooks need not be restricted to any particular cuisine because they are learning the techniques and processes rather than aiming at a particular recipe. Therefore, for them this is a better way to get acquainted with the art of cooking. Let us call it fusion technique!

In short, this section should be treated as advanced experimentation. You can follow the recipe and see if you like it; or see what is in the recipe, what processes are involved; look at what ingredients you have got and how you would like to change it.

When changing a recipe or creating something new, think outside the box. If you have a dish (either your own or bought from a shop), look at it to see the colours, feel the textures; close your eyes and smell the aroma. Think how you would like to make it, how you can improve it.

As an example of the technique of thinking outside the box, refer to the recipe for dry cauliflower in Section 23 which gave me an idea for making a hot and sour curry using cauliflower leaves, which then next day ended up as an ingredient for the Bolognese sauce for spaghetti.

In experimenting with flavours and textures think of complementary and contrasting properties: bitter and sweet, hot and sour, hot and sweet (like chilli and chocolate).

For example:

Adding pineapple pieces to many savoury dishes (especially stir-fry) produces interesting flavours.

Adding cooking apple instead of adding acidity to a dish like fruit crumble or even stews or curries.

Adding chilli flakes to chocolate cake or chocolate-based dessert; you can even try chilli chocolate bought from shops!

Using sauces likes soya sauce for cooking Asian vegetables.

The recipes in this part have come from various sources: mainly from family and friends. They are specially selected from the point of view of experimenting with ingredients and processes. Many can be changed in various ways.

There are a lot of vegetable dishes in this part. This is deliberate. The reason is these vegetables can be served with all kinds of dishes such as rice, couscous, naan, in a wrap, as a filling for sandwich, with potato mash, with grilled meat dishes etc.

A note about some of the ingredients

All the ingredients mentioned in the following pages are available either in supermarkets or in ethnic shops. Ghee is available in small cans and will last a long time if stored in a cool dry place; no need to store it in the fridge and it is worth having in your store cupboard. You can use butter or margarine instead of ghee, however you will find that ghee produces a unique flavour of its own. The various lentils (whole and split) can be obtained from supermarkets and also from ethnic shops. Fresh curry leaves are also available from supermarkets and ethnic shops, otherwise you can use the dry variety readily available from ethnic shops. Do not despair If you have not got any particular special ingredient; this is your chance to experiment using something similar in taste or smell.

HAPPY EXPERIMENTING!!

22

SOUPS, SNACKS, DIPS AND RAITAS

Soups in general

I have included only one soup recipe here because it is slightly different from most other soups. I have covered the subjects of making soups and using ready-made soups in Section 19. These are quite easy to make and serve as a light meal or lunch. You can find many soup recipes in cookbooks and on the internet.

Remember that you can improve or change the texture or flavour of the soup by topping it with a variety of things like croutons, noodles, shredded vegetables, spinach etc. We have covered this aspect before in Section 19.

Sweet potato and chorizo soup

This is quite easy to make and involves various processes like roasting and frying that are useful to practise. The soup can be frozen.

INGREDIENTS

* 400g sweet potatoes chopped into ½ inch pieces
* 125g spicy chorizo sausages chopped into ½ inch pieces
* 1 red pepper deseeded and chopped
* 1 red onion roughly chopped (about 100–125g)
* 3 or 4 cloves of garlic with skin on

- ½ inch piece of ginger cut into 2 or 3 pieces
- 450ml chicken or any other stock
- Chilli flakes (if the chorizo is not spicy) quantity as required

You should not need to add any salt or pepper to this soup, so check before adding any.

METHOD

Preheat oven to about 180°C.

Roast red pepper, garlic and ginger with a dash of olive oil in a tray for about 40 minutes.

Roast separately sweet potato and red onion with a dash of olive oil for about 50 minutes.

Fry the chorizo pieces in a frying pan with little oil. Add chilli flakes if the chorizo is not spicy. Drain the chorizo on to a tissue paper to absorb the oil.

Transfer all the roasted ingredients and the chorizo to a pan, add stock and boil for about 30 minutes.

Blitz the contents using a hand mixer, add a little water if required to make it into a smooth mixture. Strain the mixture through a sieve if it is not smooth enough.

Serve with garlic bread, toast or bread rolls.

Snacks

About snacks

This is a section that experimental cooks will find useful and most interesting. Snacks are simple to make, and the proportion of ingredients can be varied. Snacks are quite popular all over the Indian continent. They are offered to visitors anytime of the day and can be served with tea, coffee or with drinks. It is a good substitute for biscuits or cakes for these occasions. Quite often they are served as a brunch when the midday meal is planned for late afternoon. It is a good field for experimental cooks to create their own versions and new recipes.

Savoury peanuts and cashew nuts

This is a very simple and excellent snack for serving with drinks. The peanuts will disappear in minutes If you get it right (not difficult). Mango powder is made from raw green mangoes and is available in packets in ethnic shops. It gives much better flavour than citric acid.

INGREDIENTS

- ❖ 1 cup peanuts or cashew nuts (unsalted and unroasted raw variety)
- ❖ ½ cup gram flour (chick pea flour)
- ❖ ¼ tsp turmeric
- ❖ 1 tbsp garam masala
- ❖ ½ tsp mango powder or ¼ tsp citric acid
- ❖ Pinch asafoetida

❖ 1 tbsp red chilli powder (use less if you do not want it too hot)

❖ ½ tsp salt or according to taste

❖ 2 tbsp cooking oil

❖ A little water

METHOD

Put all the dry ingredients except the nuts into a bowl and mix well. Add peanuts and mix. Add the oil. Add a little water just to moisten the mixture (like thick paste). Mix well so as to coat all the nuts. Spread the mixture on a baking tray and bake in an oven at about 200°C till golden brown. You may need to stir them once or twice to roast them evenly. Let them cool down completely, when they will become crispy.

Savoury popcorn

This is actually a very simple and quick recipe. I have described this in more detail than necessary because I feel that experimental cooks can learn something new about how and why the popcorn kernels pop.

INGREDIENTS

❖ 175g popcorn kernels (you get them in supermarkets).

❖ 1½ tsp salt

❖ 1¼ tsp hot chilli powder

❖ 5 large cloves of garlic sliced

❖ 1 large clove of garlic finely chopped and crushed

❖ 3½ tbsp oil, and a few additional drops for brushing the pan.

METHOD

You need a five to six litre capacity saucepan with a lid.

Heat the oil in a small skillet or a small frying pan. **The oil should be very hot**. Add chilli powder, salt and **then** crushed garlic followed by sliced garlic. Turn off the heat after about half a minute. The crushed garlic should be dark brown (but not caramelised) and the garlic slices would be dark pink. Set aside the mixture. We will need it at the very end.

Lightly brush the base and sides of the large sauce pan. Heat the pan, it should be quite hot; you can feel the heat if you hold your palm carefully over the pan.

Add the popcorn kernels and put the lid on. Now shake the pan from time to time. This helps all the kernels to make contact with the bottom of the pan, which is where all the action takes place. Do not shake it constantly like stirring, otherwise they will not have enough time to heat.

The popping action: the inside of the kernel has a small amount of moisture locked into the fibres. The steam generated breaks open the skin and the kernels 'pop open'. If the kernels have been stored for too long they can dry out and might fail to pop properly. In which case next time you use them try spraying a little water ensuring all the kernels are evenly sprayed and leaving them for a few hours before trying. I never have needed to do this.

Coming back to our method, wait for about seven minutes while occasionally shaking the pan. You will hear the first few kernels start to pop and you can hear the sound as they hit the bottom of the lid, then quickly followed by more kernels popping. **Turn down the heat to medium**. Again shake the pan but this time at shorter intervals as the rest of the kernels have to get to the bottom and circulate through the mass of the popped ones. **This also helps to prevent the popped kernels from burning.**

Wait until the popping has died down. You can take the lid off and have a look. The saucepan should be full of pooped kernels almost to the top. Turn off the heat. **Leave lid off** to let the steam out, otherwise the popcorn will become chewy.

TOPPING

Wait till the popcorn has cooled down. This may take 25 to 30 minutes. Make a well in the middle of the popcorn and pour the contents of the chilli and garlic mixture and mix the lot with a wooden spoon. The chilli and the cloves should be evenly mixed. Have a taste; sprinkle more salt if you need.

Serve as snacks or as accompaniment to drinks.

Savoury semolina

This is an all-time favourite of our family. I have briefly covered this dish in Section 10. This is a very simple dish but due to the delicate flavours involved you may need to try a couple of times to get it right. It is a good dish for experimental cooks to learn the technique of roasting flours.

INGREDIENTS

* 100g coarse semolina

* 1 medium size (about 150g) onion chopped (not fine)

* 1½ to 2 tbsp urid daal

* 3 whole dried red chillies

* 2–3 tbsp cooking oil

* 400ml water. (You may only need between 325–375ml depending upon the semolina)

* Salt to taste

METHOD

Dry roast the semolina on low heat. The semolina will start changing colour from pale yellow to dark ivory. Turn off the heat before it becomes brown. Set aside.

Boil the water and leave it in a jug ready for use. Heat the oil in a pan and add the whole dried red chillies and urid daal. The daal will start browning quickly. Turn off the heat as it just starts becoming pink, **do not let it burn**.

Turn on heat and add the chopped onion and cook gently till it softens and becomes pink. Add the semolina and keep stirring.

Measure about 150ml of the hot water from the jug, turn on the heat to medium and add the water to the pan slowly while stirring the semolina mixture all the time. You will see that it starts swelling. Keep stirring and adding the water you have measured. At this point the semolina will have formed some globules; try to reduce them as much a possible while gently stirring all the time. Add salt to taste.

Now add the rest of the water in small amounts as above and the semolina will keep on swelling as it cooks. You may not require all the water. Stop adding water before it becomes too moist. Cook gently with the lid on for a few minutes. Sir again to break any larger granules into small ones. Taste, adjust salt. If required, sprinkle chilli flakes to increase hotness.

Serve with a wedge of lemon.

Grated savoury potatoes

This recipe works with normal potatoes and also sweet potatoes.

INGREDIENTS

- ❖ 350–400g potatoes, any type but waxy ones work better
- ❖ 1 heaped tbsp cumin seeds
- ❖ 50g (5–6 tbsp roasted peanuts) roughly pounded
- ❖ 3 tbsp ghee. (Works better with ghee, alternatively use butter or margarine)
- ❖ 2 tbsp curry leaves

❖ 4 large green chillies

❖ Salt to taste (check if using salty peanuts)

❖ Clove and cinnamon powder mixture (1 part cloves to 3 or 4 parts cinnamon)

❖ Lemon or lemon juice

METHOD

Wash, peel and grate the potatoes. Transfer the grated potato to a large bowl with cold water and leave for about 15 minutes to reduce the starch. Now using both your hands squeeze the gratings into balls about the size of an orange, set them into another bowl. Discard the starchy water remaining in the large bowl.

The next process is optional but it prevents the cooked potatoes from becoming sticky. **If you prefer to omit it then go straight to the process headed cooking.** Spread a thick tea towel on your kitchen worktop. If you happen to a have a large board use that instead. Cover the tea towel with a few sheets of clean newspaper. Break open the balls and spread the grated potatoes evenly on the sheet. It will probably make a layer of about ¼ inch thick. Spread another tea towel over this and place a flat item such as a large tray or something and put some weights on it to squeeze out the remaining moisture. Leave for about an hour, remove the grated potatoes which should be reasonably dry by now. You do not want it be too dry because you still need a little moisture in them to cook.

Cooking: Heat a large pan. Add the ghee and when it is hot

181

add the chillies, curry leaves and cumin seeds, wait for about 20 seconds till they start becoming brown, turn off the heat. Add the grated potatoes and turn the heat back to medium. Stir from time to time to ensure they are not sticking to the bottom of the pan and burning. Cook for couple of minutes then add the peanuts and cook further till the potatoes are nearly cooked. Taste and add salt if required. Cover the pan during the last five minutes of cooking to allow the steam to finish the cooking process. The potatoes should be cooked sort of al dente, slightly crunchy and not overcooked. However it is your choice how you prefer them. For an extra kick sprinkle on some clove and cinnamon powder towards the end of cooking. Serve hot with a wedge of lemon.

You can also serve this dish with a couple of tablespoon of yogurt. It adds a different flavour and also takes out some of the heat.

Grated savoury sweet potatoes

The method and the ingredients are the same, except use the same quantity of sweet potatoes. Sweet potatoes are less starchy so you can bypass leaving them in cold water, squeezing out the water and the next process of pressing out the water if you wish.

Variation: If you do not have enough potatoes or sweet potatoes add some grated carrots. They provide some extra colour and taste. There is no need to soak them in water before using.

Stuffed mushrooms

INGREDIENTS

* ❖ 8–10 medium to large size mushrooms
* ❖ 3 slices of streaky bacon
* ❖ 1 tbsp butter
* ❖ 75–90g Cheddar cheese (grated)
* ❖ 2–3 spring onions
* ❖ Salt and black pepper as required

METHOD

Preheat the oven to 200°C.

Chop the spring onions.

Dice the bacon and brown it in little oil.

Remove and chop the stems from the mushrooms and set the caps aside.

Mix the chopped stems, chopped spring onions, two thirds of the cheese, bacon and a little black pepper and salt to taste (check: the bacon might be sufficiently salty). Stuff the mixture into the mushroom caps. Transfer the stuffed caps on to a baking tray.

Bake for 15 minutes. Sprinkle the tops with the remaining cheese while the mushrooms are hot and serve.

Stuffed marrow

This is a variation of the stuffed mushroom recipe and I will leave the details for the experimental cook. You can use any soft marrow type vegetables such as courgettes, small squashes etc. Alternatively you can also use other types of vegetables such as peppers (any colour). The idea is to cut the vegetables into about 1½ inch thick pieces (if using marrow). Core the flesh out leaving a layer at the bottom intact, effectively turning the pieces into small pots. Cook the cored-out flesh with garlic, chopped onion, peas or sweetcorn and chopped green chillies or black pepper to taste. Stuff the cored vegetable pots with the cooked mixture and bake in the oven. You can try topping with cheese. If you are using peppers then slice off the top, just clean out the white bits, stuff the peppers and cap it with the top slice before baking.

Bhel

Bhel is a type of Indian street food. The word 'Bhel' means mixture. It is virtually an assembly job.

INGREDIENTS

❖ Any kind of savoury snacks sold under the name 'Bombay mix'. These are sold in many varieties in packets with names such as 'Bombay mix', 'Sev', 'Chewada', 'Sev Mummra', etc. These are made mainly from chickpea flour in a variety of flavours and sold in different shapes such as vermicelli or ribbons. There are also some varieties of savoury flakes such as rice flakes or corn flakes. Some mixes have peanuts, cashew nuts or shredded coconut in them. You want at least three to four types. You need a handful of each variety. You can also use lightly crushed potato crisps (avoid those with vinegar).

❖ Optional: A couple of handfuls of puffed rice called mummra. This is a plain variety without any spices usually available in ethnic shops in large packets. It should be crispy. If you find it has gone a bit soft or chewy, then warm it under a grill at low temperature for three or four minutes in a baking tray. Do not let it become brown.

❖ 1 medium onion finely chopped

❖ Lemon or lemon juice

❖ 5–6 green chillies finely chopped

❖ 5–6 tbsp coriander chopped (optional)

❖ Optional: Cashew nuts or peanuts, about half a cup, extra chopped coriander for garnishing.

METHOD

Mix all the dry ingredients in a large bowl. The relative proportion is not important but if you are using puffed rice (mummra) then have more of it than of the rest.

In a separate bowl, mix the chopped onion, chopped chilli and chopped coriander. Add salt to taste. Squeeze some lemon juice over and set aside.

Serve the bhel mixture in small bowls topped with the onion mixture. Traditionally a spoonful of tamarind paste is used as a topping. Garnish with chopped coriander.

Raitas

Raitas are popular accompaniment to the traditional Indian Thali, where different types of food (such as rice, vegetables, curries, pickles etc.) are served together on a plate. In Asian cuisine you may think of raitas as kind of spicy sorbet that help to clean the palate. Raitas come in different flavours like savoury, sweet and sour, hot and spicy etc., and can be made from a variety of vegetables such as cucumber, carrots, beetroot, tomato and even banana and also a mixture of these. There are two main methods of making raitas. One is to mix the chopped or shredded vegetables with yogurt and add spices (a tiny bit of coriander and cumin powder, chilli powder or chopped green chilli, salt and lemon juice to taste.) The other is to leave out the yogurt, cumin and coriander. Instead, season the raita mix with a hot oil seasoning using curry leaves or a tiny bit of asafoetida. This works best with bland vegetables such as beetroot.

The following recipes are some examples, however I would suggest experimental cooks try out their own ideas. Raitas is really a good area where nothing much can go wrong and you will learn a lot about creating different tastes. Some raitas can also be used as dips.

Beetroot raita: Two different methods

INGREDIENTS: FOR METHOD 1

❖ Cooked beetroots: You need the ready-to-eat beetroots cooked in natural juices, **not in vinegar.** They are available in small packets (3–4 whole beetroots per packet) in supermarkets. About three beetroots are plenty for this recipe.

❖   1½ tsp cumin powder

❖   2 green chillies finely chopped, or black pepper

❖   2 tbsp chopped coriander

❖   Juice of a lemon, salt to taste

ADDITIONAL INGREDIENTS FOR METHOD 2 WITH HOT OIL SEASONING

❖   5–6 fresh or dry curry leaves, 1 tsp cumin seeds, oil for seasoning

❖   Slice the green chillies instead of chopping

METHOD: 1 WITHOUT HOT OIL SEASONING

Transfer the beetroots into a large bowl, discard the red liquid. Wash the beetroots under cold water. Scrape off the rough outer layer with a peeler or a small knife. Cut them into very small pieces (smaller than ¼ inch).

Mix the beetroot pieces with chopped chilli (or plenty of black pepper), cumin powder, chopped coriander and some lemon juice and salt to taste. Serve as a side dish with a meal.

METHOD 2: WITH HOT OIL SEASONING

This is my favourite method as it tempers the sweetness of the beetroot with the flavour of the seasoning.

Peel and chop the beetroots as above.

Create the hot oil seasoning mixture as follows:

Heat a small pan or skillet, add about 2 tsp of oil and wait till it is really very hot.

Add the sliced green chillies, curry leaves and cumin seeds, wait for 4 or 5 seconds, turn off the heat and add the beetroot mixture to it, stir and turn on the heat again for about 30 seconds while stirring. Turn off the heat. Taste and add salt and lemon juice to taste.

Cucumber raita: Three different methods

This is very similar to the beetroot raita and can be done both with and without seasoning. The ingredients are the same except you also need peanuts.

INGREDIENTS: FOR METHOD 1

❖ A piece of firm cucumber about 8 inches long. If the core is too soft then spoon out the core.

❖ 1½ tbsp roasted peanuts (salted or unsalted). If using salted check taste before adding more salt. Pound the peanuts roughly

❖ The rest of the ingredients are the same as in beetroot raita method 1

ADDITIONAL INGREDIENTS FOR METHOD 2: HOT OIL SEASONING

❖ 5–6 fresh or dry curry leaves, 1 tsp cumin seeds, oil for seasoning

ADDITIONAL INGREDIENTS FOR METHOD 3: WITH YOGURT AND HOT OIL SEASONING

❖ 2–3 tbsp yogurt

METHOD 1 AND 2

Same as the beetroot raita, except add the pounded peanuts to the mixture

METHOD 3

Same as method 1 beetroot raita (without hot oil seasoning) except add the yogurt.

Tomato and onion raita: Three different methods

The recipe is basically similar to the cucumber raita method 1, 2 and 3.

INGREDIENTS: FOR METHOD 1, 2 AND 3

❖ About 3 medium tomatoes chopped in small pieces (instead of cucumber)

❖ 1½ tbsp roasted peanuts (salted or unsalted). If using salted check taste before adding more salt. Pound the peanuts roughly.

ADDITIONAL INGREDIENTS FOR METHOD 2: HOT OIL SEASONING

❖ 5–6 fresh or dry curry leaves, 1 tsp cumin seeds, oil for seasoning

ADDITIONAL INGREDIENTS FOR METHOD 3: WITH YOGURT AND HOT OIL SEASONING

❖ 2–3 tbsp yogurt

METHOD 1 AND 2

Same as the beetroot raita, except add the pounded peanuts and onion to the mixture.

METHOD 3

Same as method 1 above (without the hot oil seasoning) except add the pounded peanuts, chopped onion and yogurt to the mixture.

Grated carrot raita: two different methods

This is the most popular raita in our family. It so delicious that we serve it as a side salad or side dish with savoury rice and biryani dishes. Both the methods are simple assembly jobs.

INGREDIENTS FOR METHOD 1

❖ 4 medium to large carrots washed, peeled and grated

❖ 2 or 3 green chillies sliced (or black pepper if you prefer)

❖ 2 tbsp roasted and roughly pounded peanuts. (Taste before adding salt if using salted peanuts)

❖ Lemon

ADDITIONAL INGREDIENT FOR METHOD 2

❖ 3–4 tbsp yogurt

METHOD 1 (WITHOUT THE YOGURT)

Simply mix all the ingredients and squeeze some lemon juice. Add salt to taste.

METHOD 2 (WITH THE YOGURT)

Simply mix all the ingredients, stir in the yogurt and squeeze some lemon juice. Add salt to taste.

VARIATION TO METHOD 1:

You can try hot oil seasoning similar to the raitas above.

Hot, sweet and sour banana raita

INGREDIENTS

❖ 1 or 2 ripe bananas

❖ 1 green chilli finely chopped, or black pepper if you prefer

❖ About 3 tbsp yogurt

❖ Lemon

❖ 1 tsp sugar

❖ Salt to taste

METHOD

Peel and crush the bananas by hand, **do not squeeze into a pulp.** Add the chilli and mix in the yogurt and some juice of lemon, sugar and salt to taste.

Pachadi

We used to make this dish on our school picnics. This is basically similar to the tomato and onion raita with hot oil seasoning except you add chopped vegetables like cucumber, tiny cauliflower florets, and grated carrots. Use green chillies and season with hot oil using either cumin seeds and curry leaves or mustard seeds and a pinch of asafoetida. You need a bit stronger seasoning because of the cauliflower.

Note: scrape the outer skin of the cauliflower florets for better taste.

Chutneys and Preserves

In the West the word chutney is used for some kind of relish, or sweet and sour pickle like tomato or apple chutney. In fact in the East those preparations come under the name sweet pickles. The proper chutney is a hot preparation, usually pounded (or mixed with yogurt as in South India) and contains ingredients like herbs, daals, peanuts etc. It is usually served in small quantities or sometimes as a dip along with snacks.

Coconut chutneys:

You usually see a variety of this type of chutney served with South Indian dishes like dosa or wada. These can be white, red or green, usually with fried urid daal which gives it a nutty taste and crunchiness. These can also be served as dips or as an accompaniment to savoury snacks.

BASIC RECIPE

The authentic recipes for these chutneys calls for freshly grated coconut which involves breaking open a fresh coconut and grating the flesh; a time-consuming task. So here is how you create something very similar: in our recipes we will call this 'grated coconut'.

METHOD TO CREATE **GRATED COCONUT** FROM DESICCATED COCONUT

Put half a cup of desiccated coconut into a small bowl, pour in an equal amount of milk, mix it and let it soak in the fridge overnight. Take it out the next day. You will find most of the milk has been absorbed by the desiccated coconut and the resulting mixture should be the consistency of thick porridge. Now adjust the consistency as follows:

If it is too thin pour out the excess milk. If it looks too dry add a little more and leave it for another hour or so in the fridge. Your alternative to the grated coconut is now ready. This brings me to mention another useful trick. Very often some Indian recipes call for garnishing with freshly grated coconut. This garnish is quite useful for many savoury dishes. You can create something near the freshly grated coconut from the thick porridge like mixture. All you need to do is gently squeeze out the excess milk, stir the remaining mixture to get some air into it and leave it in the fridge for a few hours. It almost looks and tastes like the real article! You can use this for garnishing any of the savoury dishes in this book including dry vegetables.

A: Green coconut chutney

INGREDIENTS

❖ ½ cup fresh grated coconut (see method above to use desiccated coconut)

❖ 1 tbsp urid daal

❖ 1 tbsp channa daal (split chick peas)

❖ 1 or 2 green chillies finely chopped

❖ 2 tsp chopped coriander

❖ 2 or 3 fenugreek (Asian name methi) seeds

❖ ¼ tsp mustard seed

❖ A little oil for hot seasoning

METHOD

Dry roast the urid daal and channa daal separately in a hot frying pan. The time required to roast for the two daals is different, **therefore do not mix them before roasting.** Take care, it will burn very quickly, keep stirring till it turns pink.

Mix the two daals and roughly pound them, you need fine sand-like consistency, not powder.

Mix the pounded daal with the grated coconut and chopped chilli. Add salt to taste.

Add a little oil to **a very hot pan**, add the mustard seeds, as soon as they start popping add the fenugreek seeds and turn off the heat. Pour the mixture over the coconut and daal mixture and stir. Add the chopped coriander and stir lightly.

B: White coconut chutney

Same as the green chutney except leave out the chopped coriander.

C: Red coconut chutney

Same as the white chutney except use red chilli powder instead of the green chillies.

Coriander chutney

This is quite a hot type of chutney and normally only two or three teaspoons of it are served with the main meal. It will keep in the fridge for four to five days. The best way to preserve it is to freeze it as small cubes in the ice-cube tray. Fill the tray with the chutney, put it in a freezer bag and leave it in the freezer. The chutney will last for two to three months. That way you can take just one or two cubes out as required. You can also add these cubes to curry or vegetable dishes as added spice.

The method requires a wet/dry grinder. I use a small grinder, the type you see on cookery programmes. Alternatively you can use a pestle and mortar.

INGREDIENTS

❖ A couple of handfuls of fresh coriander washed and drained. Trim the roots but keep the stems.

* 1 medium size garlic clove chopped

* 2 or 3 green chillies finely chopped

* 1½ tbsp peanuts (taste before adding salt if using salted peanuts)

* 2–3 teaspoons desiccated coconut (optional)

METHOD

Finely chop the coriander (including the stems).

Grind or pound together the garlic, chillies, peanuts and desiccated coconut. Add to this mixture the chopped coriander and grind together. The consistency of the resulting mixture need not be too fine; you can decide the texture to your choice. Usually there is no need to add any water to create the paste as the coriander normally has enough moisture; but if you do want, try adding just a spoonful. The pounding method can create a dryer and rougher mixture which some prefer. The experimental cook should try both methods.

Mix the paste in a small bowl and taste before adding any salt. Squeeze a few drops of lemon juice into it.

VARIATIONS:

1. Use a mixture of mint and coriander (1/3 mint to 2/3 coriander).

2. Add a small piece of ginger to the basic ingredients before grinding.

3. Add a few pieces of sharp fruit like apple (Bramley or

Granny Smith) or raw mango. Adjust the quantity of coriander accordingly.

4. Use cashew nuts instead of peanuts.

Chilli oil

You have probably come across this in Chinese or Thai restaurants as a dipping sauce for starters. In fact it has more uses than that. It is very easy to make.

INGREDIENTS

❖ Fresh fiery hot chillies. Any very hot chillies like Thai, Jalapeño, Mexican, Tabasco, Bird's Eye, Jamaican etc. Red chillies are preferable only because of the colour. If your chillies are not of the very hot variety then add a couple of tablespoons of chilli flakes when you fill the storage container.

❖ Cooking oil: either groundnut or sunflower (do not use rapeseed or olive oil). The oil should be about 2–2½ times the amount of chillies

❖ A pinch of salt

METHOD

Chop the chillies roughly (not too fine) and add to the bottle you will use. Warning: keep your hands off your face and eyes. You can wear suitable gloves or rub some barrier cream or oil into your hands. The best way to wash your hands after chopping chillies is rub some cooking oil into your hands, add a bit of soap and rub it to create an emulsion, then wash it off and then wash your hands as per normal. **USE COLD WATER. Hot water opens up the pores in the skin and the acidic content may seep in**

and stay on the hands for a while!

Measure the required amount of oil and heat it fairly hot (about 80°C) but not so hot that it will start smoking. Let it cool completely. It might take an hour or so. Then simply add the oil to the bottle containing chopped chillies and a pinch of salt and close the top tightly. Shake the bottle and leave it for five or six days for the chillies to infuse into the oil. The oil will last a long time. You can keep topping it up with chillies and oil as required.

This oil can be used as a dip and also for sprinkling on cooked dishes, salads and soups to add extra heat and flavour. Do not use it during the cooking process as chilli; instead add it at the end of the cooking process to increase heat.

Chilli pickle

This is a simple chilli pickle recipe. It will last for up to three months if kept in an airtight jar. Store in a cool place or in the fridge. Take care in handling the chillies as explained in the chilli oil recipe above. The recipe calls for ¾ tbsp salt; this is required to preserve the pickle.

INGREDIENTS

❖ 250g green chillies washed, dried, sliced and cut into quarters

❖ Juice of two large lemons

❖ ½ tbsp mustard seeds

❖ ½ tbsp fenugreek seeds roughly pounded

- ½ tsp turmeric powder
- ¼ tsp asafoetida
- ¾ tbsp salt
- Cooking oil as required (see method); do not use olive oil

METHOD

Find a suitable glass jar: the chopped chillies should fill about three-quarters of the jar. Wash and dry the jar and set aside.

Heat about six tablespoon of oil in a skillet. The oil should be very hot. Add the mustard seed; as soon as they start popping turn off the heat and add the asafoetida and fenugreek seeds and turn the heat back on, add turmeric and turn off the heat after a few seconds. Do not let the spices burn. Set aside this mixture to cool. You will require it later.

In another pan heat about 120ml of oil to about 80°C. Set aside to cool. You will need it to top up the jar as required.

Mix the salt and turmeric with the chopped chillies and pack them into the jar. Now add the cooled oil with the seasoning and stir around with a spoon to mix it well.

Now top up the jar with the other **(plain)** cooled oil so that the jar is filled almost to the top, leaving about ¼ to ½ inch gap at the top. If you have excess oil left, put it back in its container for reuse; if you are short then repeat the process of heating and cooling some more oil and then top up the jar.

Pickled carrots

INGREDIENTS

- ❖ About 3 carrots peeled and chopped into small cubes (about 150ml in volume)
- ❖ 25–30ml cider vinegar
- ❖ 1 tsp brown sugar
- ❖ ¼ tsp paprika
- ❖ ¼ inch piece of root ginger sliced
- ❖ 1 green chilli sliced
- ❖ 1½ tsp cooking oil
- ❖ 1 tsp chilli sauce (any variety), or any other sweet and sour sauce

METHOD

Mix the vinegar, sugar and the paprika and the chopped carrots in a bowl. Marinate for 30 to 60 minutes.

Heat oil in a wok, add the ginger and add the green chilli. Add the marinated carrot mixture. Cook for a few minutes, till the carrots are slightly tender. Add the chilli sauce. Taste and add a pinch of sugar if required.

Note: Pickled carrots are not actually a pickle, it is a side dish like raita.

23

VEGETABLES, DAALS
AND MAIN MEALS

A note regarding the word 'bhaaji'

In the many Asian restaurants in the West, the word **'bhaaji'** is wrongly used in connection with a type of fried starters that should actually be called **pakoras**. The word bhaaji is actually any vegetable which could be dry or somewhat moist that is used as a side dish or as a filling such as found in masala dosa (a type of savoury pancake). I have used the word **bhaaji** in its correct sense, **'a side vegetable** dish'. There is a word **'Bhaji'** where the letter **'a'** is pronounced as **'u'** in **'curry'** which is the traditional name for pakoras in the Maharashtrian cuisine

If you do not like too spicy food then many vegetables like spinach, pak choi and courgettes can be simply stir-fried with sliced crushed garlic and thinly sliced ginger with some black pepper. However I would recommend you to try some of the recipes in this section.

Vegetables

Aubergine vegetable

INGREDIENTS
* ❖ 250–300g aubergines

- 6 large cloves of garlic sliced in half and slightly crushed (about 15g)
- 2–3 green chillies or 2 tsp red chilli powder
- ¼ tsp cumin powder
- ½ tsp coriander powder
- ¼ tsp turmeric powder (optional)
- 1–1½ tsp garam masala
- 1 tsp jaggery or sugar
- 1¼ tbsp oil
- Salt to taste.
- Chopped coriander for garnishing

METHOD:

Wash and chop the aubergine into about ½ inch wide pieces and leave in cold water with a little salt till you are ready to cook them. This takes out the bitterness and also keeps the aubergines from changing colour.

Take the aubergines out and drain just before starting to cook.

Heat oil in a pan, add the garlic and the chillies. Add the drained pieces of aubergine and sauté for a few minutes. Add the coriander powder, cumin powder and the garam masala, turmeric powder and cook for a few minutes more with the lid on until the aubergine pieces are tender. Do not overcook. Add the jaggery or sugar and salt to taste. Garnish with coriander. Squeeze a few drops of lemon over while serving.

This is basically a dry vegetable. If you prefer you can add little water when cooking with the lid on to make it moist.

Variations

1. Add chopped tomatoes during the first stage.

2. Add parboiled potato pieces during the first stage.

3. Add roughly chopped onion after adding the garlic, sauté and then add the aubergine.

Dry bhindi bhaaji

INGREDIENTS

❖ About 250–300g frozen bhindi. (These are available whole or cut. Choose the cut type). If using fresh bhindi refer to the note in the method.

❖ 2–3 green chillies sliced or 2 tsp red chilli powder.

❖ ½ tsp mustard seeds

❖ 2 or 3 fenugreek seeds

❖ ¼ tsp cumin powder

❖ ½ tsp coriander powder

❖ ¼ tsp turmeric powder

❖ 1–1½ tsp garam masala

❖ A small piece of Amsul (also called kokam) or a 1½ tsp tamarind paste or alternatively citric acid.

❖ Salt to taste.

❖ Chopped coriander for garnishing.

METHOD

Note:

1. This recipe is also suitable for using fresh bhindi but it will require washing, drying, topping and tailing and cutting into 4 mm circular pieces.

2. The addition of acidity (by using amsul or tamarind paste or citric acid) to reduce stickiness is optional; it does not make any difference to the taste but improves the appearance. Amsul and tamarind paste are available in ethnic shops. Fresh bhindi is less likely to become sticky than the frozen ones.

3. This is a dry vegetable, **do not add any water** during the cooking.

If you are using frozen chopped bhindi then defrost it thoroughly, drain the water and leave it to dry on a tissue paper before using. You can also use fresh bhindi as mentioned above.

Heat oil in a pan, add sliced chillies, fenugreek seeds and mustard, turn off the heat as the seeds pop. Add the bhindi pieces and sauté for a couple of minutes. You will note that bhindi will start to become sticky. Add the optional acidity element (amsul or tamarind or citric acid) and stir well till the sticky appearance almost clears up.

Add the cumin powder, coriander powder, turmeric, garam masala and chilli powder (if using instead of green chillies). Cook **without the lid on** till tender. Add salt to taste.

Garnish with chopped coriander.

Cabbage sambharo

This is a very simple, quick and delicious recipe. It works better with tender cabbage like pointed cabbage. It is our favourite family recipe and comes from Saurashtra, part of North Gujarat, India.

INGREDIENTS

- ❖ 1 small to medium size cabbage
- ❖ 3–4 green chillies sliced
- ❖ 3–4 fenugreek seeds
- ❖ ¼ tsp turmeric powder
- ❖ Oil for seasoning
- ❖ Chopped coriander for garnishing
- ❖ Salt to taste

METHOD

Slice the cabbage in half and soak in a large bowl for about 15 minutes. Drain and shred in very thin slices, the thinner the better because it needs to cook quickly in a few minutes. You need about four or five large handful of shredded cabbage.

Heat oil in a pan or a large skillet, add the sliced chillies and the fenugreek seeds, then add the cabbage after a couple of seconds (**do not** let the fenugreek seeds burn). Stir and sauté the cabbage. You will find the volume of the cabbage will start going down indicating it is almost cooked. Add the turmeric and salt to taste. Put the lid on and cook for a further couple of minutes, turn the heat off. The cabbage should be crispy not overcooked. Taste and adjust salt, and garnish with chopped coriander. Serve while hot.

Sweet and sour savoury cabbage

INGREDIENTS

❖ 1 small to medium size cabbage

❖ 3–4 green chillies sliced

❖ 3–4 fenugreek seeds

❖ 1 medium size onion roughly chopped

❖ 3 tbsp plain peanuts (not roasted)

❖ 3 tbsp shredded dry coconut pieces (optional)

❖ 1½ tsp jaggery or sugar

❖ 1 tbsp lemon juice

❖ ¼ tsp turmeric powder

❖ ½ tsp clove and cinnamon powder

❖ Oil for seasoning

❖ Chopped coriander for garnishing

❖ Salt to taste

METHOD

Soak the peanuts for about half an hour then drain and set aside.

Mix the jaggery and the lemon juice in three or four tablespoons of water and set aside.

Slice the cabbage in half and soak in a large bowl for about 15 minutes. Drain and chop roughly. You need about four or five large handfuls.

Heat oil in a pan or a large skillet, add the sliced chillies and the fenugreek seeds; **do not** let them burn. Add the onion and sauté till it is soft, add the peanuts and coconut pieces (if using) stir and add the turmeric powder. Add the chopped cabbage, sauté for a few minutes with lid off. Stir well and add the mixture of jaggery and lemon juice and cook for a few minutes more with the lid on. Stop cooking when the cabbage is just soft and cooked. Sprinkle with a little water if required. Taste and add salt if required. Sprinkle with the clove and cinnamon powder and stir. Garnish with chopped coriander.

VARIATIONS

1. Use cashew nuts instead of peanuts, no need to soak them.

2. Add peas or sweetcorn, adjust the quantity of cabbage to suit.

3. Use readymade sweet and sour sauce with a little water instead of the jaggery and lemon juice mixture.

4. Garnish with desiccated coconut and coriander instead of using shredded coconut.

Dry cauliflower bhaaji
and how to think outside the box to create something new

INGREDIENTS

- ❖ 250g small cauliflower florets
- ❖ 4 tsps of oil
- ❖ 2–3 green chillies
- ❖ 2 tsp mustard seeds
- ❖ ¼ tsp turmeric (slightly more if you prefer)
- ❖ Pinch of asafoetida
- ❖ ½ tsp sugar
- ❖ Chopped coriander for garnishing
- ❖ Salt to taste

METHOD

Pinch out or cut off tiny florets from the cauliflower about 5 or 6mm diameter pieces. You want small florets because the small size will allow them to be coated with the spices and also cook in a short time. Size matters!

Add oil to the hot pan and wait till the oil heats up; it should be really hot. Add mustard seeds and green chillies, put the lid on and turn the heat off or down very low to stop the mustard seeds from burning. (Putting the lid on prevents oil splashes as the seeds pop up). Put the heat back on and add a pinch of asafoetida immediately followed by the cauliflower florets. If you are concerned about burning the asafoetida then turn the heat off again and add the florets.

Turn on the heat, add turmeric, and a couple of tablespoons of water to generate the steam, stir and put the lid on. Cook for about three to four minutes on medium heat.

Add the sugar and salt to taste. Cook with lid off while stirring to prevent burning for a minute or so. Add the garnish. Turn the heat off and keep the lid on.

The bhaaji should be ready in a couple of minutes. You can taste and add more heat if required by adding chilli flakes.

About the experiment (thinking outside the box)

Part I: *Cauliflower leaves*
When I cooked this vegetable recently I found that there were some fleshy leaves that I could do something with. This is what I did.

Discard any dry leaves. Peel the skin off the leaves to expose clean fleshy inside. Chop finely the fleshy parts and also good fresh green leaves. You then need finely chopped tomatoes, about 1½ times the volume of the chopped leaves. The tomatoes should be fresh and slightly sour in taste. Mix the leaves and tomatoes.

OTHER INGREDIENTS
* 2 tsp ghee (ghee works best here but you can use butter)
* 1½ tsp cumin seeds (cumin seeds and tomato always work very well for flavour)

* 2 tsp urid daal (adds crunchy and nutty flavour, as there is nothing much else in the ingredients in this recipe)

* 2 large green chillies, sliced (if you have no fresh chillies then use dry whole chillies, not powder; or add chilli flakes later on)

* Salt and sugar to taste

METHOD

Heat the ghee; it should be fairly hot. Add the chillies, urid daal and cumin seeds and in a few seconds (just long enough for the cumin to start browning, do not allow it to burn) add the cauliflower leaves and tomato mixture, stir and cook for two or three minutes. Add enough water to **just** cover the mixture, not more at this stage, you can adjust the amount later. Cover and cook till the mixture become tender. Taste, add salt and a little sugar.

You are looking for a hot and sour mixture of the consistency and looks of a thick red soup cum curry. Adjust water and then taste to your requirements. If required cook for further for a couple of minutes. It tastes delicious and can be frozen and reheated.

Part II: Bolognese sauce

I had quite a bit of this curry cum soup left. I could have turned it into a lovely tomato soup by blitzing it with a hand mixer. However, I had some cooked spicy pork mince in the freezer which gave me another idea.

I mixed the mince and the curry/soup and used it as a sauce

for spaghetti Bolognese the next day.

Dry potato bhaaji

This is a very simple and quick bhaaji and besides having it as a side dish it can also be used as a filling in wraps, sandwiches etc. This works best with ghee; alternatively you can try margarine or butter **but not oil.**

INGREDIENTS

* ❖ 4–5 medium size potatoes
* ❖ 2 tsp cumin seeds
* ❖ 1 tbsp ghee
* ❖ ½ tbsp black pepper
* ❖ Salt to taste

METHOD

Wash and peel potatoes. Cut them into about ½ inch or slightly smaller cubes. Leave them in a bowl of cold water till you are ready to cook to stop them becoming discoloured. Drain them just before starting cook.

Heat the ghee in a pan. The ghee should be very hot. Add the cumin seeds and wait for a few seconds till they just start changing colour. Turn off the heat, add the potatoes and turn the heat on again. Sauté the potatoes for a few minutes while stirring well, **ensuring that they do not burn.** Add the black pepper and a little salt. Cook further for a few minutes with the lid on till the potatoes are cooked. It will take only two three minutes, avoid overcooking. Taste and add salt and more black pepper if required.

Spicy potato bhaaji

This spicy potato bhaaji is similar to the one you find in many Indian restaurants and takeaways. It is moist and you can adjust the consistency of the sauce to your choice.

INGREDIENTS

❖ 4–5 medium size potatoes, boiled and skinned and left in cold water

❖ 1 medium to large onion finely chopped (you want about half the quantity of the potatoes)

❖ 3–4 green chillies chopped finely

❖ 3 tbsp finely chopped coriander

❖ 1½ tsp garlic and ginger paste (60:40 proportion)

❖ 1½ tsp mustard seeds

❖ 1 large tomato chopped into small pieces

❖ ½ tsp turmeric

❖ Pinch of asafoetida

❖ ½ tsp garam masala

❖ ½ tsp sugar

❖ Salt to taste

METHOD

Using a small grinder or pestle and mortar, make a paste using the chillies, coriander, garlic and ginger paste. Set aside.

Cut the boiled potatoes into ½ inch pieces. Set aside.

Heat oil in a pan. Add the mustard seeds and just as they start popping add the asafoetida and turn off the heat. Add the chopped onions turn on the heat and add the turmeric. Cook the onions till soft. Add the boiled potatoes pieces and cook for a couple of minutes. Add the chopped tomato and the garam masala. Cook with the lid on for a further minute. Taste and add sugar and salt as required.

VARIATIONS

Add vegetables such as peas, cauliflower, diced of carrots etc. Adjust quantity of potatoes to suit.

Mushrooms in cream and butter sauce

This is a popular side dish served in restaurants with steak or fish dishes. Note that mushrooms do not require much cooking; the process described here makes them crispy and buttery.

INGREDIENTS

For the mushrooms
❖ About 15–20 small button mushrooms

- 4–5 cloves of garlic, halved and crushed

- 3 tbsp butter

- Black pepper as required

- Salt to taste

- Juice of half a lemon

For the sauce

- 50ml white wine

- 100ml double cream

- 40g butter

- Juice of half of lemon, use as required

METHOD

1. Make sauce first

Melt the butter using a microwave or a hob. Set aside.

Reduce the white wine in a small pan by gently simmering for four to five minutes. Reduction intensifies the flavour.

Add the double cream and butter to the reduced wine and simmer until it thickens (like thin porridge). Set aside.

2. Heat the wok to a high temperature. Add the butter, when melted add the garlic wait for a few seconds and add the mushrooms. Gently toss the wok so that all the mushrooms get coated with the butter and shake the pan from time to time for a couple of minutes only. **Do not stir using a spoon or similar.** This is important because bruised mushrooms will become watery and soggy, we want the mushrooms to remain crisp. Sprinkle plenty of black pepper while frying the mushrooms. **Do not overcook** the mushrooms.

Reduce the heat, pour the cream sauce over the mushrooms continue cooking for another 30 seconds. Add the lemon juice and salt to taste. Do not cover, serve hot.

VARIATION:

Instead of making sauce just use a mixture of double cream and little milk.

Green beans two ways

Simple quick green beans: The beans should be crisp and al dente when cooked.

INGREDIENTS

- ❖ About 125g fresh or frozen tender green beans
- ❖ 1 tbsp butter
- ❖ 3 garlic cloves, halved and crushed
- ❖ Black pepper as required
- ❖ Salt to taste

METHOD

Wash and drain the beans. (If using frozen beans, thoroughly defrost.) Top and tail the beans, and set them aside without chopping.

Heat a wok or frying pan. Melt the butter and add the garlic. Let the garlic turn pink and add the beans, sprinkle black pepper and sauté for two minutes, put the lid on and cook further for one or two minutes. Turn off the heat. Add salt to taste.

Spicy green beans

Note: This recipe calls for ajwan (or ajmo) seeds (known in the West as carum seeds or seeds of Bishop's weed). They add a spicy, hot and pungent flavour to the dish. They are easily available in ethnic shops and worth the trouble for the experimental cook to try and use. Alternatively, use cumin seeds instead.

INGREDIENTS

❖ About 125g fresh or frozen green beans

❖ ½ tsp ajwan seeds or cumin seeds

❖ 1½ tsp hot paprika or 1 tsp red chilli powder

❖ 1 tbsp of dark soya sauce

❖ 2 tsp cooking oil

❖ 2 tsp margarine

❖ Salt to taste

❖ Pinch of sugar

❖ Chopped coriander for garnishing (optional)

METHOD

Wash and drain the beans. (If using frozen beans, thoroughly defrost.) Top and tail the beans, and set them aside without chopping.

Heat wok to a high temperature, add the oil and margarine. Add the ajwan or cumin seeds, wait for a few seconds and add the beans. Sauté the beans for a couple of minutes, put the lid on and cook till the beans are tender. Add the paprika or chilli powder, soya sauce and a pinch of sugar and mix well. Taste and salt as required. Garnish with coriander.

VARIATION

Cook the beans using one of the spice bases with or without onion and without ajwan seeds or soya sauce.

Daal varieties

Masoor (red lentils) daal

Note: This recipe is based on masoor daal (red lentils). However you can also use the same recipe for moong daal (yellow lentils). These are available in most supermarkets and in ethnic shops. Besides using them as daals you can also add them to home-made soups and stews (like adding pearl barley) to add extra flavour and body, so it is worth keeping a stock.

The churning stick mentioned in the method can be obtained from ethnic shops and is quite useful for mixing liquids. It consists of about 10 inch long wooden rod with about 1 ½ inch diameter and ¾ inch thick star shaped end. I have also seen them on the internet. It makes the daal more homogeneous. However it is not necessary if you do not have one.

Amsul or tamarind paste adds acidity and flavour; you can use lemon juice instead.

INGREDIENTS

❖ 60–65g masoor daal washed and soaked for 2–3 hours in cold water

❖ 3–4 garlic cloves halved and crushed

❖ ¼ tsp mustard seeds (optional)

❖ 5–6 curry leaves

❖ 1 medium onion roughly chopped

❖ 1 medium to large tomato finely chopped

❖ 2 whole dry red chillies. Alternatively 1¼ tsp red chilli powder

❖ 2–3 fenugreek seeds

❖ Pinch of asafoetida

❖ ¼ tsp turmeric powder

❖ ½ inch piece of amsul or ½ tsp tamarind paste (or you can use 1 tsp lemon juice)

❖ 1 tbsp of cooking oil

METHOD

Drain the soaked daal and set aside.

Heat oil in a pan. Add the whole red chillies (do not add the chilli powder at this stage if you are using it instead of the whole chillies), curry leaves and fenugreek seeds, wait for a few seconds and turn off the heat. Turn the heat on, add a pinch of asafoetida and add the onions. Cook the onions till pink and add turmeric powder and stir. (If using mustard seeds add them just after the fenugreek seeds.)

Add the red chilli powder (if using) and add the daal, mix well and sauté the mixture till daal is tender. Do not let it go dry and burn; add a couple of tablespoons of water if required. Add the chopped tomatoes, about 100ml of water and cook the daal with the lid on till it is soft. You do not want too much water at this stage.

At this stage you can make the daal mixture a bit more homogeneous by using a hand held churning stick or blender. It is not absolutely necessary, so you can omit this stage and continue.

Add the amsul or tamarind or the lemon juice and a pinch of sugar. Taste and add salt as required. Simmer for 2 to 3 minutes.

Now the daal is ready. You can add more water according to your preference before serving. It can be frozen for later use. In that case do not add more water; you can do this after defrosting.

VARIATIONS

1. Use the recipe with yellow moong daal and green moong daal.

2. Use the smoking technique to give a smoky flavour.

3. Garnish with caramelised onions.

Taraka daal

'Taraka' is a sort of hot oil seasoning poured over the finished daal. Basically it consists of finely chopped onion, cumin seeds and a small piece of whole dried red chilli. However some people add curry leaves and garlic cloves also. The taraka adds distinctive flavour to the daals.

TO MAKE THE DAAL

Cook any daal (red lentils, yellow lentils etc.) in the same way as the masoor daal recipe above. Omit the curry leaves if you are using caramelised onions.

INGREDIENTS FOR THE TARAKA:

- ❖ 2 to 3 tsp cumin seeds
- ❖ 3 to 4 cloves of garlic
- ❖ 1 whole red or green chilli (sliced if using green chilli)
- ❖ ½ tbsp. oil
- ❖ ¼ inch piece of ginger (optional)
- ❖ A few curry leaves

❖ For the garnish, one small onion finely sliced and caramelised (optional instead of curry leaves).

TO MAKE THE TARAKA

Heat the oil in a small pan. When the oil is **very** hot add the taraka ingredients, wait for a few seconds, turn off the heat, pour the hot taraka over the cooked daal and stir lightly.

Optional:

Garnish with caramelised onions.

Add chopped tomatoes

Rice varieties

Note: as mentioned earlier in the book rice is a very versatile ingredient (even more so than potatoes). The method of cooking rice is given in full detail in Section 12. Once you have mastered the art of cooking rice you can experiment and create your own recipes. Below are a few ideas. You can serve rice with dishes from Asian as well as Western cuisine instead of potatoes (roasted, mash or chips); or serve rice on its own with chutney, raita or pickles. There are many excellent pickles available in the supermarkets.

The recipe ideas in this part start from simple rice moving on to a bit more involved ones like the biryani.

Simple savoury rice

This is the simplest version. All you do is cook the rice as described in the recipe section using the Type 1 base seasoning described in Section 10.

BASIC STEPS

Use the type 1 base (with or without onion). Add some turmeric powder and chilli flakes. Throw in a few raw peanuts and then add the soaked rice and cook. You can try green peas or sweetcorn if you like.

Bacon rice

This is a lovely dish created by my wife and has been a family favourite.

INGREDIENTS

- ❖ 80g Basmati rice
- ❖ Water for soaking the rice: about twice the volume of rice (refer to Section 12)
- ❖ 55g smoked bacon rashers
- ❖ 40g green peas
- ❖ 50g roughly chopped onion
- ❖ 1½ tsp cooking oil
- ❖ Pinch of salt

METHOD

Measure the volume of dry rice. Wash and soak the rice for about 2 hours as per the detailed steps in the Section 12, and set aside.

Trim the excess fat from the bacon rashers and cut them in about ¾ inch wide strips and again cross wise so that you end up with pieces about ¾ inch square. Exact size is not important.

Heat oil in a pan, add the onions and sauté for a couple of minutes, add the bacon pieces and fry for a further two or three minutes till the bacon is almost cooked. Do not let the bacon burn or turn crispy and brown as served with bacon and eggs; we want the bacon almost cooked and soft.

Spoon in the soaked rice avoiding the water as much as possible, stir the rice and the onion and bacon mixture for a few seconds and then add any leftover rice and the water. Add a pinch of salt. Add the peas and stir.

Cook the rice exactly the same way as the rice recipe.

Aubergine rice

FOR THE AUBERGINE FILLING

❖ 1 tsp red chilli powder

❖ ¼ tsp cumin powder

❖ ½ tsp coriander powder

❖ 1 tsp garam masala

- ¼ tsp jaggery or sugar

- ¼ tsp salt

- ½ tbsp oil for frying

- 60-70g aubergine

FOR THE RICE

- 80g basmati rice

- Water for soaking the rice: about twice the volume of rice (see Section 12)

- Pinch of salt

METHOD

Measure the volume of dry rice. Wash and soak the rice for about 2 hours as explained in Section 12, and set aside.

Make the aubergine filling.

Wash and chop the aubergine into about ½ inch wide pieces and leave in cold water with a little salt till you are ready to cook them. This takes out the bitterness and also keeps it from changing colour.

Take the aubergine out and drain just before starting to cook.

Heat oil in a pan, add the chopped aubergine pieces, cumin powder, coriander powder, garam masala, chilli powder, jaggery (or sugar) and the salt. Sauté for three or four minutes.

Spoon in the soaked rice avoiding the water as much as possible. Stir in the rice and the aubergine, then add any remaining rice and the water. Add a pinch of salt. Cook the rice as per the rice recipe.

VARIATIONS

This is a typical recipe for savoury vegetable rice. You can try this recipe with many other vegetables such as cauliflower, peas, carrots etc. Try adding onion either roughly chopped or chopped into small cubes. You will find that the onion taste different according to the way it gets cooked and according to the shape.

Masoor sooji

The word 'sooji' ('soo' pronounced as 'sow' in 'sowing') is used to describe savoury rice containing lentils. This is a dish from Maharashtra State in India. Basically it is made from soaked whole masoor (whole red lentils, not the split ones). These are readily available from ethnic shops and some supermarkets.

INGREDIENTS

- ❖ 75g basmati rice

- ❖ Water for soaking the rice: about twice the volume of rice (refer to the Section 12)

- ❖ 35g whole masoor (whole red lentils). Requires soaking overnight.

- ❖ 1½ tsp garlic and ginger paste

- ½ tsp coriander powder
- ¼ tsp cumin powder
- 2 tsp red chilli powder
- ½ tsp turmeric powder
- ½ tsp cinnamon and clove powder (1 part cloves to 3 to 4 parts cinnamon)
- Pinch of asafoetida
- 1 medium onion finely sliced
- ½ tbsp oil for frying
- ¾ tsp salt

METHOD

Wash and soak the lentils (masoor) **overnight** in cold water. Drain and set aside in a bowl.

Measure the volume of dry rice. Wash and soak the rice for about 2 hours as explained in Section 12, and set aside.

To the lentils add garlic and ginger paste, the coriander and cumin powder, chilli powder, turmeric powder, and the cinnamon and clove powder. Mix all together.

Heat oil in a pan, add the onion and fry till pink, add the lentils and spice mixture, and the asafoetida and stir and sauté for three to four minutes till the lentils are tender. Make sure that the spices do not sick to the bottom of the pan and burn. When the lentils are cooked add the salt. Spoon in the soaked rice avoiding the water as much as possible. Stir in the rice, then add the any remaining rice and the water. Cook the rice as per the rice recipe in Section 12.

Optional: Garnish with freshly grated coconut or coriander.

Savoury fried rice

This is a simple, delicious dish and is a family favourite. The interesting thing about it is that it is always made from leftover rice or rice cooked and left for at least five to six hours to cool. Since it is usually made from leftover rice, there is no exact proportion of the ingredients. The following is a guide but you can vary the proportions to your taste and according to the quantity of rice available.

INGREDIENTS

❖ About five large handfuls of cooked rice

❖ 5–6 cloves of garlic, sliced

❖ 2–3 green chillies, sliced

❖ ½ tsp turmeric powder

❖ 1 tsp mustard seeds

❖ 1 medium onion (about 70g) roughly chopped

❖ 1 tbsp cooking oil

❖ 6–8 curry leaves, fresh if possible, use otherwise dried leaves

❖ 1 tsp salt

❖ 4–5 tbsp chopped coriander for garnishing

❖ Lemon slices

METHOD

If the rice has been in the fridge, take it out and transfer it into a larger bowl, and rub it by hand to separate the grains and make it free of lumps. Leave it out for a while to get rid of any condensed moisture.

Add half of the salt and half of the turmeric to the rice and mix well.

Heat the oil in a large skillet or pan, add the chillies, curry leaves, garlic and lastly the mustard seeds. As soon as they start popping, turn off the heat, add the chopped onion and turn the heat back on. Fry till it turns turn pink.

Add the rest of the salt and turmeric powder, stir and add the rice. Stir well for three to four minutes to heat the rice all the way through. Cover the pan and heat thoroughly on a low heat for a further three to four minutes, make sure it is not burning, stir from time to time. Garnish with chopped coriander and a slice of lemon and serve hot.

VARIATION

1. Add peas.

2. Savoury bread: you can use the same recipe to use leftover stale bread or naans. Break the bread slices or naan into small crouton-size pieces. Follow the recipe, but add four to five tablespoons of chopped roasted peanuts to the onions. Adjust salt if using salted peanuts.

Italian style aubergine rice

My wife used to cook this dish. Unfortunately she did not write down the recipe. I have recreated the dish as near as possible to the original flavour in my memory. This is another example of experimenting. It should taste a bit sour which goes well with the aubergines and the Italian herbs. You can adjust the quantity of vinegar according to its strength and your palate. You can also vary the proportion of rice to aubergines.

INGREDIENTS

❖ 250g cooked rice

❖ 60g onion roughly chopped

❖ ¼ tsp chilli flakes

❖ 150g aubergine

❖ 2 large cloves of garlic (about 10g) sliced

❖ 2–3 tsp red wine vinegar

❖ Cooking oil as required

FOR THE MARINADE

❖ 40 ml red wine vinegar

❖ ¼ tsp brown sugar

❖ ¾ tsp paprika

❖ ½ tsp black pepper

❖ ½ tsp olive oil

❖ ½ tsp Italian dried herbs either a ready-made mixture or make a mixture of:

❖ ¼ tsp dried basil

❖ Pinch of dried tarragon

❖ Large pinch of dried thyme

METHOD

Mix all the ingredients of the marinade together.

Wash and slice the aubergines lengthwise in thin slices (about 4 mm thick). Cut them again across in about 1½ inch wide pieces. Add the pieces to the marinade and mix well.

Heat 1½ tsp oil in a pan, add the garlic, add the marinated aubergines and sauté for a couple of minutes. Sprinkle on a little water and cook further for three to four minutes with the lid on. Turn off the heat when the aubergine pieces are soft, then drizzle ½ tsp vinegar to bring back the acidity lost in the cooking. Add a pinch of salt.

Heat oil in another pan, fry the onion till it is light pink, add the chill flakes and cooked rice. Mix well add salt to taste. Drizzle ¼ tsp vinegar and mix.

Mix the aubergines and rice. Add more salt or vinegar if required.

Meat And Fish Recipes

General note about meats:

Although the following recipes are based on specific a type of meat you can use any meats such as lamb, chicken, turkey, pork, beef, shellfish etc. You can even use processed meats such as pork sausages (just chop them into large cubes). The structure and the natural flavour of different types of meats vary, so you will need to adjust the cooking process and change around some of the ingredients or their proportions. For example pork is bland; its flavour is enhanced by adding acidic ingredients like vinegar or sweet and sour fruit like pineapple. Shellfish requires only few minutes to cook and needs a minimum of spices; just some garlic, chilli and a pinch of masala is enough. Chicken can be made into curry or dry cooked in the oven using the same type of masala or readymade tandoori masala paste. You can also try ingredients from a different cuisine; for example try soya sauce or red or white wine, barbeque sauce etc. For creating the sauce you can use water, coconut milk, stock cubes, readymade stock, canned thick soups such as tomato soup or mushroom soups etc. You can add any vegetables, for example leaf vegetables like spinach or others like cauliflower, broccoli, carrots, potatoes, canned sweetcorn, corn-on-cob pieces etc. Another thing you can do is to mix the meat with pasta, noodles etc.

You can also experiment using fresh herbs like dill, tarragon, fennel and sage. Dill and tarragon are particularly delicate herbs that go with fish, shellfish and chicken.

However before experimenting and making any changes I

231

would advise that you try using the recipe as described.

Meat biryani

Note about biryani: biryani is basically a dish with succulently cooked meat (usually lamb but you can use chicken or prawns) mixed with deliciously cooked rice with a smoky flavour. The rice grains should be moist but separated and not coated with the sauce. It is an ancient dish developed by the Moguls. In parts of India such as Hyderabad, you can have many varieties of biryani. The biryani that one gets in most western Indian restaurants is nothing like the real article but a simple version of savoury rice mixed with meat. You can also have vegetable biryani but it lacks the real taste of meat biryani.

My recipe comes from traditional Muslim families passed on through generations. It involves smoking of the finished dish (as described in detail in Section 10) at the end, which gives the dish its typical aromatic and rich flavour.

Biryani is ideal for the experimental cook because if you can cook rice and meat properly then it is simply an assembly process. The total experience of creating this dish will stretch you a bit and take you out of your comfort zone; but you will find it worth the effort. Once you have learned the basic recipe you can create lots of simple variations using other meats, shellfish or vegetables (freshly cooked or from leftovers).

INGREDIENTS

- ❖ 300g good quality basmati rice
- ❖ 900g diced lamb, mostly in about 1 inch cube pieces with some bony pieces from ribs.
- ❖ 750g onion
- ❖ 200g thick yogurt
- ❖ 1 tbsp ginger and garlic paste
- ❖ ½ tsp turmeric powder
- ❖ 1½ tsp chilli powder
- ❖ ¾ tsp coriander powder
- ❖ ½ tsp cumin powder
- ❖ ¾ tsp garam masala
- ❖ ½ tsp cinnamon and clove powder
- ❖ 1½ tbsp fresh mint chopped, alternatively 2 tbsp dried mint leaves
- ❖ 5 tbsp ghee
- ❖ 125g almonds
- ❖ a large pinch of saffron
- ❖ ½ inch piece of cinnamon
- ❖ 2 green chillies
- ❖ Pinch of asafoetida
- ❖ 1½ tsp lemon juice
- ❖ 2 tsp oil
- ❖ Salt to taste

METHOD

Cut cinnamon stick in to two or three pieces.

Chop green chillies finely.

Roughly chop the fresh mint. If you do not have fresh mint then soak and drain the dried mint leaves or alternatively use mint sauce.

Finely chop 75g of onion and then finely slice the rest of the onion. Set it aside.

COOK THE RICE:

Wash and soak the rice as described in Section 10 (Rice), add a tablespoon of ghee to the heated pan and add the pieces of cinnamon and then the rice. Cook the rice as described in Section 10. You want the rice to be cooked moist but the grains separated (not sticking together). Control the amount of water and sprinkle or spray water as required towards the end as described in Section 10. When cooked, cover and set aside.

MARINATE THE MEAT:

You can do this while the rice is soaking.

Mix together: Ginger and garlic paste, green chillies, red chilli powder, coriander powder, cumin powder, garam masala, turmeric powder, and two tablespoons of yogurt. Mix the meat pieces thoroughly and set aside for about half hour.

FRY THE SLICED ONION:

Heat about 1½ tsp of oil in a large frying pan and fry the sliced onion on low heat and keep stirring till the onion starts become pink, then slowly brown and starts to caramelise. The onion should appear dark but not greasy. If you cannot handle the whole amount of onions in one go then divide it in two or three lots with just a little oil to fry them. The onions will take five to six minutes to become caramelised. Place the caramelised onions in a dish lined with paper tissue to absorb any excess oil.

COOK THE MEAT

The meat should be cooked so that it is succulent and thoroughly cooked and only little moist. When the meat is removed from the marinating dish add about three tablespoon of water to the empty dish and mix all the spice residue and set aside. This will be added to the meat during cooking.

Heat three tablespoons of ghee in a pan. Add the chopped onion, fry till golden, add a pinch of asafoetida, add the marinated meat. Turn the heat to medium and stir the meat so that the spices do not burn. Sauté the meat for three to four minutes. Add the spicy water from the marinade. Add ½ tsp salt. Cover to generate steam and cook on low heat. Check from time to time whether the spices are burning; if the meat is dry and still needs cooking, add a little water and continue cooking. When the meat is cooked, taste and add more salt as required, sprinkle the cloves and cinnamon powder and simmer on low heat for a minute and set it aside.

MAKE THE SAFFRON MILK

You have probably seen chefs sprinkling strands of saffron onto the dish. This not the correct way to transfer the aroma of saffron to the cooked dishes. (Saffron is sprinkled normally only on cold and hot drinks). The correct method is as follows:

Pour about two tablespoons of milk in a small bowl. Heat a very small frying pan, add the strands of saffron and warm them on very low heat for about 45 seconds. Remove from the pan from the heat. Slightly crush the strands with the back of a large spoon. You want the strands to break into smaller pieces but not to turn into powder. Do not waste any saffron sticking to the spoon. Mix this in the milk and stir.

PREPARE THE ALMOND GARNISH:

You can do this in advance the day before and leave the almonds in the fridge.

Blanch the almonds in hot water, peel the skin, and split them in half. Using a small sharp knife slice each half lengthwise in three long pieces. Set aside.

MIX THE COOKED MEAT:

Mix together the remaining yogurt with chopped mint, half of the saffron milk and a 1½ tsp juice of lemon. Pour this over the cooked meat and mix thoroughly. Set aside.

ASSEMBLE THE BIRYANI:

Transfer the cooked rice into a large pan. Using your hands break up any lumps so that the grains are separated. Pour a couple of teaspoons of melted ghee into the rice and mix well.

Take a large microwave-proof glass bowl with cover. It should be large enough to accommodate the rice and the meat mixture leaving about an inch of space at the top for the smoking process. Start filling the bowl layer by layer. The bottommost layer should be the cooked rice. Then follow this with a layer of meat topped with few pieces of fried sliced onion. Continue layering till the bowl is almost finished. Sprinkle pieces of the sliced almonds in between the layers, leaving a quarter for the top layer. Mix the last bit of remaining rice with the left over moist gravy and spice mix from the meat. This will be the last layer. Top this layer with the remaining fried onion and almond pieces and drizzle the remaining saffron milk over it. Cover the bowl and set aside till you are ready to serve. (After the smoking and reheating process).

SERVE THE BIRYANI

Follow the smoking process described in Section 10. Remove the charcoal and the dish containing the charcoal and warm the biryani in a microwave oven. It should be piping hot. Serve with one of the raitas, especially the carrot raita in yogurt described in this section.

STORING

You can store the biryani for a couple of days and reheat when serving. Biryani freezes well and will keep for a few weeks.

Kheema (minced meat)

The following recipe is based on minced lamb, but you can use lamb, beef, pork or turkey mince.

INGREDIENTS

- ❖ 450g minced lamb
- ❖ 2 medium onions, about 175g, finely chopped
- ❖ 2 green chillies, sliced
- ❖ 1½ tsp garlic and ginger paste
- ❖ ½ tsp turmeric powder
- ❖ 1 tsp coriander powder
- ❖ ½ tsp cumin powder
- ❖ 1 tsp garam masala
- ❖ ½ tsp cinnamon and clove powder (for sprinkling at the end)

- ❖ 1½ tbsp cooking oil
- ❖ ½ tsp juice of lemon
- ❖ 3–4 tbsp chopped coriander (optional)
- ❖ 2 tbsp of yogurt (optional)
- ❖ Salt to taste

METHOD

Mix the garlic and ginger paste with all the dry ingredients excluding cinnamon and clove powder. If using yogurt mix this in as well.

Mix the mince and the spice mix together. Set aside.

Heat the oil in a pan, add the sliced chillies, add onion and fry till golden brown.

Add the mince. Fry for a few minutes on low heat so that the spices do not burn. Add a little water, cook with the lid on to produce a fairly dry mince. Sprinkle on the cinnamon and clove powder. Add a little water or little oil or ghee if required. Mince does not take more than a few minutes to cook. Taste and add salt if necessary.

Once you have the basic mince you can make it more moist or produce some gravy by adding more water. The dry mince is particularly useful for freezing and then using as a curry (with more liquid) or as a base for Bolognese sauce. You can also 'morph' it by adding peas, spinach etc.

Simple mutton

<u>INGREDIENTS</u>

* 300g diced lamb
* 75g onion, finely chopped
* 2–3 green chillies, sliced
* 1½ tsp red chilli powder
* 1 tsp ginger and garlic paste
* ¼ tsp turmeric
* ¾ tsp coriander powder
* ½ tsp cumin powder
* 1 tsp garam masala
* 4 tbsp yogurt
* 2 tsp tomato purée (optional for adding to the meat later)
* Salt to taste

<u>METHOD</u>

Mix the yogurt with all the spices except the green chillies. Add this to the meat and mix well and set aside.

Heat oil in a pan and add the green chillies and the onion till golden brown. Add the meat with the spices and fry for a few minutes taking care not to burn the spices. If required add a little water. When the meat becomes slightly brown add just enough water to cover the meat and cook with the lid on. When the meat is tender, taste and add salt as required. Add the tomato purée and simmer for another two or three minutes.

SLOW COOKING METHOD

For cooking in a slow cooker follow the method above but, instead of continuing to cook on the hob with the lid on, transfer it to the slow cooker. Cook on the automatic setting (if you have one) for up to four hours, otherwise follow the instructions for your cooker. Check and adjust the seasoning towards the end.

VARIATIONS

1. Add potatoes with the onion.

2. Add chopped canned tomatoes instead of tomato purée.

3. Brown the meat cubes in oil or ghee to a deep brown colour first, then add the yogurt mix and follow the same recipe. This gives the meat a richer flavour. Add some finely sliced deep-fried onions as a garnish.

Spicy chicken korma

INGREDIENTS

- ❖ 1 kg chicken pieces, preferably drumsticks and thighs
- ❖ 2 large onions, about 150g, finely sliced
- ❖ 1 tbsp garlic and ginger paste
- ❖ 1 tsp coriander powder
- ❖ ½ tsp cumin powder
- ❖ 2 tsp chilli powder

- ❖ 2 cardamoms (preferably green ones) roughly pounded
- ❖ 150ml yogurt
- ❖ 2 tbsp oil
- ❖ 2 bay leaves (optional) for frying with the onion
- ❖ Lemon juice
- ❖ Tomato purée (optional)
- ❖ Salt to taste

METHOD

Wash and dry the chicken. If you can, take the skin off the drumsticks and thighs by pulling it off using a soft cloth; otherwise leave it.

Mix the yogurt, garlic and ginger paste, and all the dry ingredients except the cardamoms and bay leaves. Rub the yogurt mix into the chicken pieces.

Heat the oil in a pan, add the bay leaves and the onion and fry the onion till golden brown, add the cardamom and then the chicken and fry for a few minutes. Add enough water to cover the pieces and cook with the lid on till tender. Taste and add salt as required. Add a few drops of lemon juice. Add tomato purée (if using) and simmer for two or three minutes.

Meat korma

INGREDIENTS

- ❖ 400g diced lamb

- ❖ 3 medium onions, finely sliced

- ❖ 60g yogurt

- ❖ 2 tsp garlic and ginger paste

- ❖ Small piece of cinnamon

- ❖ 6 cardamoms

- ❖ 4–6 black peppercorns

- ❖ 2 tsp cumin seeds

- ❖ 2 tsp chilli powder

- ❖ 1 tbsp fresh/dry mint leaves (optional)

- ❖ 1 tbsp almond flakes (optional)

- ❖ 2 tbsp oil

- ❖ Salt to taste

METHOD

Pound together all the dry ingredients (except the almond flakes) and the mint leaves. Mix together this pounded masala, the garlic and ginger paste, the chilli powder and about three tablespoons of yogurt and chopped mint leaves, set aside.

Wash and drain the meat. Rub the masala mixture into the meat and marinate for about half an hour. Heat the oil in a pan and fry the onion till golden and soft. Add the meat and fry for a few minutes till light brown. Do not let the spices burn. (Sprinkle on a little water if required). Add the remaining yogurt a little at a time while stirring and cooking the meat. Add a little more water just to cover the meat and cook till tender with the lid on. Add salt to taste.

When cooked add the almond flakes and simmer for a few minutes.

Slow cooker ideas

Cooking curries, stews and soups with a slow cooker is nothing different from cooking on a hob. You just transfer the process to the slow cooker for further processing. You will need to cook the meat four to five hours depending upon your cooker and the setting. The advantage here is that it will not burn.

Always start off by going through the first stage up to frying the onion and browning the meat and the transfer it to the slow cooker. For the gravy you can add either stock made from stock cubes, or canned soups like tomato soup or mushroom soup. You can even add items such as spinach or other vegetables halfway through the cooking.

You can also use slow cooking for further tenderising the meat from your curry.

Here are some more ideas:

Goulash

You will find plenty of recipes for goulash on the internet and in books. Basically you will need either lamb or beef cubes, red and green peppers, canned chopped tomatoes (or thick tomato soup), smoked paprika, and sour cream.

Season the meat, add the ingredients except the stock or the soup and cook for a few minute and transfer to the slow cooker. Add the stock. Check and adjust the flavour halfway through the cooking.

Meat cooked in mushroom sauce

This is similar to the above except use thick mushroom soup instead of tomato soup. You can change or adjust other ingredients according to your taste.

Simple dry fish curry

This fish curry has no sauce, it is cooked in tomato sauce and topped up with green leafy vegetables like fresh fenugreek or spinach.

INGREDIENTS

* 200g cod fillet
* 100g tomatoes, finely chopped
* 100g onion, finely chopped
* 1 tsp ginger and garlic paste
* 1 tsp coriander powder
* ½ tsp cumin powder
* ½ tsp turmeric powder
* 2½ tsp red chilli powder
* Salt to taste
* 2 tsp lemon juice
* 1 tbsp oil

❖ 100g roughly chopped fresh fenugreek or spinach leaves. You can use frozen chopped spinach but defrost it before using.

METHOD

Partially cook the green leaves (fenugreek or spinach) in the microwave oven for two or three minutes. Set aside.

Mix together the ginger and garlic paste, coriander and cumin powder, chilli powder, turmeric and the lemon juice. Wash and cut the fish. Rub the paste onto the fish fillet and set aside.

Heat the oil in a pan, add the onion and fry till golden brown. Add the chopped tomatoes and cook till they are soft. Add the fish pieces and cook over a low heat for a couple of minutes till the fish becomes opaque. Top up the fish with the partially cooked green leaves, put the lid on and cook for another two minutes on a very low heat. Turn off the heat add salt if required.

Simple fish curry with gravy

This recipe requires coconut milk to produce the sauce. It is available in shops in small cans.

INGREDIENTS

❖ 200g fish fillet (cod or haddock)

❖ 1½ tsp ginger and garlic paste

❖ 4–5 large cloves of garlic, crushed and sliced

❖ 2½ tsp chilli powder

- ½ tsp turmeric powder
- 1 tsp lemon juice
- 200ml coconut milk (see alternative below)
- 1 tbsp oil
- Salt to taste

METHOD

Wash the fish. Remove the skin if you prefer, otherwise leave it. Cut the fillet into about 2 inch pieces.

Mix the garlic and ginger paste, chilli powder, turmeric powder, lemon juice and a pinch of salt. Rub it into the fish, set aside.

Heat oil in a pan, add the crushed garlic and let it become pink. Add the fish, fry on both sides for a minute. Add the coconut milk, put the lid on and simmer without stirring on a low heat for two to three minutes. Depending upon the size of the fillets, the fish should have cooked by now. Check, taste and add salt if required.

If you do not have coconut milk you can use desiccated coconut instead. Soak about 100g of desiccated coconut in sufficient milk to cover the coconut overnight. (Milk should be about twice the volume of the coconut). Most of the milk will soak in. If possible use a blender to make a homogeneous mixture. Use this in place of coconut milk. The sauce will not appear quite as smooth because of the desiccated coconut.

As an alternative sauce, use chopped tomatoes blended in a blender.

Pastas and pies

Savoury vermicelli with kheema

This is a very simple but delicious dish. The recipe came to us from a South Indian friend, but I think it originates from Parsee or Zoroastrian cuisine. It requires vermicelli which is different from the thin rice noodles. You can get it in supermarkets or in ethnic shops. Asians use it to make savoury and also sweet dishes. Ensure to get the roasted variety.

INGREDIENTS

❖ 100g vermicelli (roasted variety)

❖ 75g dry cooked lamb kheema

❖ 1 tbsp sultanas

❖ 2 tbsp chopped onion

❖ 2 tbsp ghee for frying the vermicelli (you can use oil instead)

❖ 1½ tsp oil for the onions

❖ 2 bay leaves or 4–5 curry leaves

❖ 2 whole dried red chillies, slightly crushed

❖ 60ml (approximately) water

❖ Slice of lemon

❖ Salt to taste

METHOD

Note regarding kheema: the recipe calls for dry cooked lamb kheema. Cook the kheema as per the kheema recipe in this section but only use just enough water to cook. Dry out any remaining water by frying on low heat.

Cut the vermicelli into about 2 inch pieces using kitchen scissors. Note that the vermicelli is quite brittle and crunchy and the pieces tend to fly about. Use a large bowl to catch any flying pieces. Heat the ghee in a pan and fry the vermicelli till it is light pink in colour. Note that it can burn quite easily, so you will need to keep it stirring. If required divide the quantity in half and fry half the amount at a time. Set aside.

Heat 1½ tsp oil in a pan, add the whole chillies, the bay leaves or the curry leaves and the chopped onion. Fry till the onion is soft and pink. Add the cooked kheema, and a couple of tablespoons of water, stir well and fry to warm it thoroughly. Test and add salt if required. Turn off the heat.

Now add the fried vermicelli and mix well with the kheema. Add the sultanas. Turn on the heat and cook the vermicelli with the lid on. You will need to sprinkle or spray a **little** water from time to time to generate and maintain the steam. The vermicelli should be soft but not soggy. It will take only few minutes to cook. Serve hot with a slice of lemon.

Shepherd's pie

For this recipe you need cooked kheema and mashed potatoes. Ideally, use good waxy potatoes. Boil and mash the potatoes, add some butter, black pepper and little milk and mix well to produce a soft, slightly savoury and buttery mash.

Fill a greased ovenproof pie dish with the cooked kheema and top it with the mashed potatoes. You can choose the relative proportion of kheema to the mash; I like 50:50. Bake it in the oven. Serve hot with any gravy.

Toad-in-the-hole with gravy

INGREDIENTS

FOR THE TOAD

❖ 6 pork sausages, or you can use 10 chipolatas

❖ 1 tsp oil

FOR THE BATTER

❖ 80g plain flour

❖ 2 eggs

❖ 250ml skimmed milk

❖ 1 tsp black pepper

❖ Salt to taste

FOR THE GRAVY

❖ 1 onion, finely chopped

❖ ½ tbsp oil

❖ 2 tsp plain flour

- ❖ 1 tsp English mustard
- ❖ 1 tsp black pepper
- ❖ 2 tsp soya sauce
- ❖ Pinch of salt
- ❖ 250–300 ml stock (you can make this using stock cubes)

METHOD

You need to fry the sausages; they should be **sizzling hot** when you pour the batter onto them. If you are roasting the sausages then preheat the oven to 220°C, gas mark 7.

Make the batter first

Thoroughly mix the flour and the beaten eggs. Add the milk a little at a time while stirring with a fork. Add the black pepper. Beat the mixture until it is smooth. Set aside.

Put the sausages in a baking tin large enough to accommodate the sausages and the batter. Remember that the batter will rise when baked. Pour a little oil on the sausages and bake in the oven for 15 minutes. Alternatively fry on the hob till they are brown and then transfer to a baking tin.

Pour the batter onto the sausages in the baking tin and cook in the oven at 220°C, gas mark 7, for 30 minutes. The batter will rise and become golden brown. Remove from the oven.

Make the gravy

Fry the onions in oil till brown. Add the flour, mustard, black pepper, soya sauce and fry till the flour is cooked. Add the stock and cook while stirring till the gravy is smooth and thick to your taste.

Serve the toad-in-the-hole with the gravy and any vegetable dish.

Macaroni in cheese sauce

This is quite a simple dish. Macaroni is quite easy to cook. Simply boil it in water with a little salt. You will need approximately 70g of dried macaroni per person.

Below is the general-purpose recipe for the basic pouring sauce that you can convert to other types of sauce such as cheese sauce.

The basic pouring sauce

INGREDIENTS

❖ 15g butter

❖ 15g plain flour

❖ ¼ tsp salt

❖ ¼ tsp black pepper

METHOD

Melt the butter in a pan. Add the flour and cook over a low heat while stirring for two minutes. **Do not allow**

the mixture to become brown, control the heat as required. Gradually add the milk and blend it in while stirring. Simmer gently, keep stirring and cook till the sauce comes to the boil and starts to thicken. Simmer for another two or three minutes. Add salt and pepper to taste. Once cooked you can adjust the consistency of the sauce by adding a little milk. You do not need the sauce to be too thick at this stage because we will be baking the assembled dish in the oven to finish off.

Cheese sauce

Make the basic sauce, add about 40–50g of any grated cheese, some Cayenne pepper or smoked paprika while the sauce is hot.

Transfer the cooked macaroni to an ovenproof pie dish. Pour the sauce onto the macaroni and sprinkle some paprika or red chilli powder over the top. Place the dish in the oven and bake for a few minutes at 180°C, gas mark 4. In addition you can brown the top by placing under a hot grill for a couple of minutes.

Spaghetti and Bolognese

Spaghetti is probably one of the easiest dishes to cook and one of the most rewarding.

INGREDIENTS

❖ Spaghetti or linguine pasta, about 90g per person

❖ Olive oil

- ❖ Parmesan cheese for grating on the top
- ❖ Bolognese sauce, about 250ml or more according to taste

Weighing/measuring pasta

The easiest way to measure or weigh spaghetti is either to bunch it up in your hand or weigh it using scales. As a guide, ten-inch-long pasta when bunched up to 2 cm diameter will weigh about 100g. The easiest way to weigh the pasta is to put a tall glass on your scales, zero them then put the pasta into the glass.

METHOD:

Boil water in a large pan. The amount of water should be enough to completely cover the pasta and rise about two or three inches on top. Keep a large colander ready in the sink and a bowl for the cooked pasta by your side.

Add some salt to the water. Add the pasta when the water starts boiling. You will need to slowly push down the pasta into the pan so as to immerse it fully. For a medium texture (not too al dente and not too cooked) cook for 12 minutes **with the lid off.** Check it by taking out a strand and tasting. Give it a bit longer if you need. **DO NOT OVERCOOK.**

Pour the water with the pasta into the colander and drain. Immediately transfer the pasta to the bowl and drizzle some olive oil and fork it. Take it straight to the table and serve with any sauce such as Bolognese or any other you like and grated hard cheese such as Parmesan.

Bolognese sauce

You can use ready-made sauce. However I use cooked kheema (see recipe above in this section) just as it is, or add partly cooked smoked bacon pieces and cook it with some extra tomatoes or tomato paste. Actually, you can use any spicy mixture; even leftover stir-fry, suitably improved with added tomatoes to make it sweet-hot and sour. Traditionally the sauce has a smoky flavour which is due to the smoked bacon.

Note:

In some Bolognese sauce recipes you will not find any bacon.

Instead of lamb you can use any mince such as beef or pork...

Breads

Refer to Chapter 16, Breads

24

DESSERTS

Sheera

INGREDIENTS

- ❖ 100g coarse semolina
- ❖ 60g white granulated sugar
- ❖ 20g sultanas
- ❖ 3 tbsp ghee
- ❖ 350ml water
- ❖ Pinch of saffron
- ❖ 2–3 tbsp milk

METHOD

You will notice that the method is very similar to the savoury semolina for the first part of the recipe.

Boil the water and leave it in a jug ready for use.

Heat the ghee in a pan. It should be fairly hot. Add the semolina and keep stirring. The semolina will start changing colour from pale yellow to dark ivory. Do not let it become brown. Turn off the heat before it becomes brown.

Measure about 125ml of the hot water from the jug, turn on the **heat to medium** and add the water to the pan **slowly** while stirring the semolina mixture all the time. You will see that it starts swelling. Keep stirring and adding the water you have measured. At this point the semolina will have formed some globules, try to break them down as much a possible while gently stirring all the time. Add the sultanas.

Now add the rest of the water in small amounts as above and the semolina will keep on swelling as it cooks. Dissolve the sugar in a little water and add to the semolina. Keep adding the water and stirring the semolina as it swells. You may not require all the water. Stop adding water before it becomes too moist. Cook gently with the lid on for a few minutes. Stir again to break any larger granules into small ones.

The sheera is now almost ready. Taste to see if it is cooked. The next stage is optional but it does give the dish an aromatic flavour.

Adding saffron

Add a couple of tablespoons of milk to a small bowl or ramekin.

Take about ten strands of good quality saffron and place them into a small frying pan and warm them for a couple of minutes, slightly crush them using the back of a large spoon. Then add them to the milk, and stir slightly, making sure you do not lose the strands sticking to the spoon. Add the mixture to the semolina and mix with a fork.

Serving sheera

This is a very popular dish over most of the Indian continent and can be served any time of the day as a snack or as a dessert. It can be served hot or cold. You can garnish it with wedges of mandarin. You can also add a little milk and serve it as a soft pudding, which tastes better hot than cold.

Sweet Vermicelli

You can make a sweet version of the vermicelli very similar to the savoury one described in Section 23. Instead of the savoury ingredients, just add caster sugar or honey or sugar syrup and some sultanas. Garnish with almonds or saffron milk.

Flapjacks

This recipe was given to us by my granddaughter, Jzuee, when she was about twelve. It just goes to prove that you are never too young to start experimenting.

INGREDIENTS

❖ 100g margarine

❖ 50g golden syrup

❖ 75g sugar

❖ 75g rolled oats

METHOD

Prepare a greased baking tray 18×25cm.

Preheat oven to 180°C, gas mark 4.

Melt the margarine, syrup and sugar in a pan and stir well.

Stir in the oats, turn off the heat and mix well.

Transfer the contents into the baking tray and flatten down with a wooden spoon.

Bake in the oven for 20 to 25 minutes till the top looks brown.

Let the tray cool for three to four minutes and cut the contents into about 20 pieces.

When cold, remove the pieces from the tray into another container.

Simple baked cake

If you have never made a cake, try this recipe. It is halfway between a cake and a pudding and requires no special skills or equipment.

INGREDIENTS

❖ 175g self-raising flour

❖ 85g unsalted butter

❖ 85g caster sugar

❖ Pinch of salt

❖ 1 large egg

❖ 5–6 tbsp milk

<u>METHOD</u>

Preheat the oven to 190°C, gas mark 5.

Prepare a greased pie dish.

Sift the flour using a sieve into a bowl. Add the salt. Using your fingers rub the butter into the flour to a smooth texture.

Beat the egg and mix it with the milk and sugar. Add the mixture to the flour, mix thoroughly using a fork. Pour the mixture into the pie dish and bake on the middle shelf for 15 minutes. Reduce the temperature to 160°C, gas mark 3 and bake for a further 35 to 40 minutes. Check if the cake is cooked by inserting a skewer, which should be clean when you take it out.

Serve with ice-cream or custard.

<u>VARIATIONS</u>

Try adding broken nuts, or use vanilla or orange essence to change the flavour.

Walnut cake

This is my wife's recipe and has been a family favourite. You will need some kind of mixer or blender to mix the butter and sugar. Although an electric blender or mixer is better for this job it is possible to do it with a hand whisk;

however you will find it a bit of a hard job.

Baking a cake looks complicated but it is not difficult. Those experimental cooks who have been following this book should be able to manage it. Do not despair if you do not succeed the first time, try again; it is an art worth mastering.

INGREDIENTS

* 175g butter
* 175g caster sugar
* 3 eggs
* 225g self-raising flour
* 85g chopped walnuts
* 1 tbsp milk

METHOD

Leave the butter at room temperature to soften.

Using a sieve sift the flour into a bowl. Set aside. Sifting makes the flour fluffy and aerated.

Prepare a greased, lined 7 inch diameter round baking tin (loose bottomed or springform).

Preheat the oven to 165°C, gas mark 3.

Keep ready some sort of cooling stand on which you can place the baked cake to cool.

Take a large mixing bowl. Mix the butter and sugar and blend it to a cream. This might take five to ten minutes depending upon the equipment you use.

Beat in the eggs one at a time while still whisking and beating. **This process is important so that the creamy mixture does not become soft and liquid.**

While still beating fold in the flour, milk and walnuts. The whole mixture will now look like a very soft dough. This might require another five to six minutes depending upon your equipment.

Transfer the mixture into the baking tin. Smooth the top with a palette knife or similar. Now holding the tin in both of your hands **bang the tin** on the work surface about three times. This ensures that there are no pockets of air left in the dough. **This step is very important for baking the cake with a good spongy texture.**

Bake the cake for 1¾ to 2 hours on the middle shelf. Observe the progress through the glass window of the oven **but do not open the oven till the cake is risen well and has started to brown; otherwise the cake will collapse.** Towards the end check if the cake is ready by testing with a skewer. Pierce the cake in the middle; the skewer should come out clean without any sticky dough on it. If required continue baking for a few more minutes and check again.

When ready, take the tin out and leave it to cool for some time. Remove the cake from the tin and place on the cooling stand.

Orange cake

This is very similar except it is made with orange juice and the zest of an orange.

ADDITIONAL INGREDIENTS (REST SAME AS WALNUT CAKE EXCEPT OMIT THE WALNUTS)

❖ Zest of an orange

❖ 120–150ml orange juice (the pulpy juice with juicy bits sold in cartons or bottles)

❖ ¼ tsp orange essence

METHOD

If using real oranges, use good quality sweet oranges and squeeze the juice. If using the thick orange juice from cartons then use the thicker part of the liquid, it gives more flavour. Add the orange essence to the juice.

Follow the recipe for the walnut cake. Add the juice after adding the eggs. Then continue the rest of the recipe as per the walnut cake.

Fruit crumble

Fruit crumbles are very easy to make and can be made with different fruits. This is an excellent area for the experimental cook to try and create their own versions. The recipe below uses apples. But you can use any other soft fruit like plums, gooseberries, blackcurrants, damsons and even rhubarb, but grapes do not work well with this recipe. You can also use a mixture of these fruits. You will need to adjust the sugar according to the acidity of the fruit mixture. It is not necessary to soften the fruit if it is quite soft.

You can sprinkle the mixture with porridge oats, nuts etc. to give a crunchy texture.

Apple Crumble

INGREDIENTS

- ❖ 400g apples (mixture of sweet and sharp apples like Bramley)
- ❖ 175g self-raising flour
- ❖ 85g unsalted butter
- ❖ 80g caster sugar
- ❖ 1½ table spoon porridge oats (optional)
- ❖ ½ inch piece of cinnamon
- ❖ Small piece of star anise (optional)
- ❖ 1 tbsp granulated sugar (for the topping)
- ❖ ½ tbsp lemon juice

METHOD

Break the cinnamon into two or three pieces

Prepare a greased pie dish.

Preheat oven to 180°C, gas mark 4.

Wash, peel, core and cut apples into ½ inch pieces. Heat three tablespoons of water in a pan. Add the cinnamon pieces, the star anise and the sugar. Mix, then add the apple pieces. Simmer with the lid on over a very low heat for about two to three minutes till the apples are slightly soft and moist. You may need to add a little water if necessary . Add the lemon juice. Taste and add some more juice if the apples are not sharp enough.

Sift the flour into a bowl. Rub the butter into it by rubbing with your fingers. Break any fatty lumps coated with flour to reasonably smooth texture. Add 75g sugar (leaving the rest or the topping) and mix thoroughly.

Transfer the cooked apples into the greased pie dish and top it with the flour mixture, pressing it down to fill all the voids between the apple pieces. Sprinkle the oats and the rest of the sugar on the top. Bake in the oven on the middle shelf for about 45 minutes till the top looks brown.

Serve with ice cream or custard.

Something naughty but nice for you to experiment with

You do not have to make deserts from scratch. Here are a few interesting ideas.

Turn chocolate biscuits into a dessert – I like to use softer biscuits like Jaffa cakes.

Place a biscuit in an individual dessert serving bowl or

plate. Drizzle a couple of spoonfuls of orange liqueur like Cointreau, Grand Marnier or Curaçao, top it with some satsuma segments and serve.

For variation you can try using crème fraîche or ice cream and other fruit. You will find that your packet of chocolate biscuits will vanish very quickly!

FURTHER EXPERIMENTATION:

If you have followed the book so far, you can learn a lot more by experimenting with your own ideas. Here are a few suggestions.

Salads soups and vegetables
Try making different salads using different ingredients and dressings.

Try chopping the salad leaves and vegetables in different shapes and thicknesses; you will find that the resulting taste changes.

Experiment with croutons, nuts, sweetcorn in soups and salads.

Try various canned beans for making soups, or adding to other vegetable dishes. Baked beans in particular can be made into an excellent spicy dish with just a few spices.

Try using different sauces for vegetable dishes instead of or in addition to the spices.

Main meals

Experiment with different pies by using different meats and mashed potato.

Experiment with stir-fries with different noodles, vegetables and meats.

Add sweetcorn to meat and stir-fry dishes.

Mix dry-cooked daals with rice to make sort of savoury rice. (See biryani)

Desserts

Try making crumble with different fruits.

Try adding nuts or porridge oats to baked deserts like crumbles.

PART V: REFERENCES

25

THE CHEMISTRY OF COOKING

In part I we have seen that our kitchen has many different chemicals. When you are cooking, various reactions take place and these chemicals react with each other, changing shape, structure, taste etc. In this section we will look at some of these chemicals in more detail. This will help you to understand the basic chemistry behind those changes and reactions. This is important for those experimental cooks who want to know why certain foods need to be cooked in a particular way or why some of their recipes did not turn out as they hoped. Furthermore, it will also help you to be more experimental when trying your own recipes.

The information is not intended to be a lesson in chemistry, food technology or biology. We are only concentrating on the properties of these chemicals from the point of view of cooking, with some essential reference to their function in our daily diet.

Before we begin it would help to understand just a few terms that are used in this section.

Refer to figures 25A, 25B and 25C; Illustrations

Molecule: Is a group of two or more atoms linked together by sharing electrons in a chemical bond. Molecules are the fundamental components of chemical compounds and are the smallest part of a compound that can participate in a chemical reaction.

Bond: This makes the various atoms join together to form a molecule. You could visualise that every atom has a greater or lesser ability to connect to other atoms, which could be of the same type or a different type. Another way is to imagine that these atoms have extensions ending with either one or more 'sockets' or one or more 'balls'. An extension with a socket from one atom can grab another atom that has a ball on its extension and join with it (like a ball and socket joint). In this way an atom with several sockets can join up with several other atoms with balls. For example water is chemically called H_2O which means that two hydrogen atoms and one oxygen atom have joined to make a molecule of water. In this example the oxygen atom has two 'sockets' and the hydrogen atoms have one 'ball' each.

The above description is an oversimplification for the sake of understanding. In reality the bonding between the atoms is more complex and involves sharing of electrons. **Refer to figure 25C.**

Note: The molecules do not remain in isolation. They, in turn, share their bonds with other molecules of the same or many different types of molecule and form a complex three-dimensional structure. As we shall see later, these structures undergo various changes during the processes of cooking, such as kneading the dough, baking, boiling, freezing etc.

The basic chemicals we will look at

Please note that although these are separately listed for the purpose of describing their properties, in the ingredients used for cooking these chemicals, together with others, normally occur in combination with other chemicals. What happens to them during the cooking processes depends upon their combination and makeup.

Proteins: (Refer to figures 25D, 25E, 25F and 25G); Illustrations

We get our proteins from the meat of animals and fish and also from plants: vegetables, cereals and pulses. Proteins are special molecules made up by joining together many amino acids, and there are a great many different proteins made from combinations of different amino acids. Proteins are essential for all our life's processes.

Gelatine is a type of tightly bound protein in its dry state. When dissolved in water the strands unravel but still remain joined together to form what we call jelly.

Proteins are constantly used up by our bodies and need to be replaced on a regular basis. The function of each protein depends upon its structure and shape, which in turn depends upon the sequence of the amino acids it is made from. During digestion the proteins are broken down into their constituent amino acids, which are transported to various organs and tissues via our blood stream. There the cells reconstitute any particular protein needed using the amino acids.

In their natural state, proteins are tightly coiled up within other molecules such as starch molecules. When heat (such as in cooking) or shear force (like beating an egg) is applied the chains become loose and form strands or structures. This is called **denaturing**. In the case of egg, with more heat the egg becomes a solid structure.

For our purposes proteins come in two main types: water loving or hydrophilic, and water hating or hydrophobic depending upon the type of amino acids it contains. Corn flour is almost pure starch and as such dissolves in liquids and is commonly used for thickening sauces.

The behaviour of a protein in contact with liquids (water, oils, melted butter, milk etc.) largely depends upon the amino acids it contains. When water or another liquid is added to a protein it absorbs some of the liquid. The liquid breaks down the molecular barrier that brings the amino acids into action. Further action depends upon the makeup of the protein and the cooking processes, such as temperature etc. Water-loving protein will dissolve in the liquid and help to thicken it. Therefore water-loving proteins are good for thickening sauces. On the other hand, water-hating proteins (generally associated with flours like plain flour) will separate from the water in the liquid. When heated these proteins form strands due to denaturisation and interact with the fat in the liquid. This results in a thick glutinous mass that we love as gravy.

Carbohydrates and starches
This group of chemicals includes simple and complex carbohydrates, starches and fibre, which are all produced

by plants. Carbohydrates are our body's primary source of energy. Essentially these are our body's fuels. There are two basic types, the simple ones consist of single molecules like natural sugars and refined sugars. The more complex ones are starches that are found in various plant foods like rice, potatoes, wheat, yams etc. Most of the carbohydrates are broken down to glucose during digestion, some are processed in the liver. Glucose is burned to produce energy. Any excess is stored as fat and in the liver for later use.

As the name suggests carbohydrates are essentially biological molecules made of carbon, oxygen and hydrogen.

Simple carbohydrates: in the simplest form these exist as sugars which plants produce to store their energy.

Starches: Starch is a bland type of carbohydrate. These rather complex molecules are made by plants in the form of small granules that contain the carbohydrate molecule surrounded by different types of proteins.

From the point of view of cooking, the behaviour of starches is of particular interest to us. Starch is basically bland and is present in grain flours and also available in pure form. The starch molecules consist of long threads that plants pack into small, tight, dense granules. During the cooking process these unwind and release the long threads from these granules in the presence of liquid (water, sauces, milk etc.).

The problem is that the granules made by different types

of plants such as corn, wheat, potato, arrowroot etc. have different structures and so behave differently. This is because the starch granules also usually have protein molecules covering them. The behaviour of these coatings depends upon the makeup of the proteins, and that depends upon the amino acids they are associated with.

In the cooking process the starches play a vital part as thickening agents for sauces, gravies and stocks. We will have a look at this in the later part of this section.

Fibres

This is the common name for another type of carbohydrates that plants produce for building their walls and inner structures. This type of carbohydrates contain cellulose, gum and pectin. Certain plants, like barley and oat, produce soluble fibre that helps to slow down absorption of sugar.

Pectin

Pectin is a bland carbohydrate whose long molecules thicken jams and jellies. Pectin is a soluble dietary fibre and has no calories. However it does help to move the food through the digestive tract.

Enzymes

Enzymes are **active** proteins that change other chemicals around them and in so doing affect the structure and flavour of foods. They may add to the flavour or in some cases, such as in fish, they can impart a mushy texture or an unpleasant taste. The discoloration of overripe fruit is due to the action of enzymes it contains, which also results in loss of the vitamins in the fruit.

Oils and fats

Oils and fats are chemicals in which animals and plants store their energy. Unlike proteins or carbohydrates these are fluids and provide delicious moistness to food. Butter and animal fats are solid at room temperature while oils are liquids. Oils are produced from different plants such as peanut, corn, rape seed, olives etc. They have different flavours and different boiling temperatures.

Saturated fats are those that are solid at room temperature because they have a more rigid structure than unsaturated fats: their saturated chemical bonds do not readily react with oxygen. The consequence of this is that they are less prone to becoming rancid. (Butter is an exception which can get rancid due to its water content, unlike ghee, which is clarified butter that does not go rancid).

Unsaturated fats are liquid at room temperature and more prone to becoming stale.

Hydrogenated fats are unsaturated fats which have been chemically modified to make them more stable and resistant to staling. Mixtures of oil and fats suspended in water or other liquids are called emulsions.

The chemistry of cooking processes

Have you ever wondered why steak can be cooked in a few minutes in a frying pan but a leg of lamb takes a long time in the oven? Why overcooked meat becomes tough but slow-cooked stew is deliciously soft? Why the Chinese slice their meat in a particular way and cook it in a few minutes? Why gravy can have lumps? Why bread requires kneading and cakes do not? You are about to find out.

As mentioned before in the opening section, experimental cooking is all about learning a bit of science behind the cooking processes. In this way you do not have to follow a particular recipe exactly. You can change the ingredients or their quantities, use a different method or process or, indeed, make up your own recipes. Understanding the science improves your ability to experiment by understanding what is going on.

We shall look at the science involved in some of the commonly used recipes and processes.

Comparison of cooking methods

Grilling

Grilling involves high temperatures and is done either under a grill (electric or gas) or in a thick pan. The surface in contact with the pan or exposed to the heat from the grill is cooked much faster than the inside part. This cooks the food by browning the surface and by using the steam generated from the inside part of the food. This is most suited for steaks, burgers or sausages.

Usually grilling requires no or very little oil or fat.

Deep-frying

The food is completely immersed in the oil or fat at a very high temperature. Deep-fried food often has a batter or coating that becomes golden brown and crispy while the inside is moist due the steam generated while frying.

Shallow-frying

This is a process in between grilling and deep-frying. The food is cooked in a frying pan surrounded by a small amount of hot oil. The food needs to be turned over to cook both sides. I would advise the experimental cook to try shallow-frying instead of deep-frying where possible. It is healthier, less messy and you do not need to worry about the leftover oil. Just wipe the pan with a tissue paper before washing in warm water.

Slow cooking

Slow cooking is basically cooking food in a thick pot with a lid at a very low temperature for a long time. Although you can cook slowly at low temperatures using a suitable pot, for best results I would recommend an electric slow cooker with three temperature settings (usually high, low and auto). The temperature range is normally between 65°C and 85°C and cooking times between three and six hours. I use a slow cooker all the time for making soups, stews and curries. The meat turns out tender and delicious, and you do not need to stand over the pot to ensure that the food does not burn. We shall see later in this section why food cooks this way in the slow cooker.

Baking and roasting

These processes require use of an oven. The position of the food, the temperature of the oven and the cooking time is dependent on the type of food, size or weight (as in the case of roasting meat), and the mixture in the bake when baking bread or cake etc.

Sometimes the temperature of the oven is changed part way through the process to allow the inside part of the food to cook and to brown off the top, or the other way round. Some bread recipes call for putting a tray of water in the oven during the first few minutes while baking to create a moist atmosphere in the oven. Roasting is sometimes done with food wrapped in cooking foil or covered in some way, and the covering then removed towards the end to brown the surface.

Steaming

Steaming is suitable for cooking food that benefits from moisture as well as heat. It is commonly used for puddings. You can use pressure cookers or purpose-made steamers to cook.

Steaming at atmospheric pressure produces delicious vegetables. There are purpose-made steamers but one can also use some sort of sieve (not plastic) with a cover on top of a pan of boiling water. A Chinese steaming basket is handy for all sorts of recipes.

Microwave cooking

Microwave cooking works by using microwave radiation to heat the moisture in the food by exciting the water molecules. Therefore it is suitable for foods that have some water content in them. Otherwise you have to sprinkle some water to create the same effect.

Although a microwave is a very useful piece of equipment and some people use the microwave for cooking most of their food, in my opinion it is better suited for warming and reheating or cooking ready meals. Apart from warming and reheating, I also use it for boiling potatoes and for making jacket potatoes. In my view the way in which food is heated makes a difference to the texture and therefore to the taste of the food. I think for experimental cooks there is more to experiment and learn by using other traditional methods.

What happens to the food during cooking?

Cooking meat

General Information about meat

Meats from different animals have **a different combination** of water, protein and fat as shown in the table below, and therefore **different cooking methods** and temperatures are used to cook these meats. The figures in the table are an average; the actual value may vary for different parts of the same animal. Different cuts of meats have different combination of muscles that consists mainly of protein fibres and connective tissues (those connect the muscles to the bones and also bind muscle fibres together) that consist mainly of collagen.

AVERAGE PROTEIN, FAT AND WATER CONTENTS OF VARIOUS MEATS			
TYPE OF MEAT	PROTEIN %	FAT %	WATER %
BEEF AVERAGE	18	22	60
BEEF SIRLOIN STEAK	26	7	67
CHICKEN	23	14	63
COD	20	1	79
HAM	15	9	76
LAMB	26	18	56
LOBSTER	22	3	75
MUSSLES	17	2	80
PORK	15	23	62
SALMON	20	13	67
TURKEY	20	varies between 2 and 7	73- 78
VENISON	35	6	59

Cook tough meats at high temperature for a longer time to dissolve the connective tissues, while tender meats should be cooked at moderate temperature so as to retain the juices and keep the meat tender.

You can find information on the exact temperature and time for roasting various meats in cookery books or on the internet. However, in general most meats require roasting between 180 – 195°C for about 30 minutes per pound or 500 grams of weight. Times will differ somewhat depending on the position of the meat in the oven, whether or not you have wrapped it and a little on your particular oven. You will learn to adjust the published timings and temperatures as you go along. It is best to check the meat nearer the set time to ensure that it is not undercooked or overcooked. Pierce the meat in the thickest part; when the skewer is taken out any juice coming out should be clear without any red in it.

Cooking steaks

The colour of the cooked steak depends upon how it is cooked. The colour will change from pink to red and then finally grey as the steak cooks from rare to well done. It is best to aim at cooking the steak from medium rare to medium which suits most people's taste. Well done steak can be quite tough and chewy. Ensure that the pan or griddle is really hot before starting. The steak should be at room temperature before putting on to the griddle and should be turned over occasionally to ensure both sides are cooked. Normally it should not take more than six to eight minutes to cook depending upon its size.

Leg of lamb

The leg should be cooked on the bone to ensure that it will retain its moisture. Follow the guidelines that come with the pack. Marinate the lamb or simply rub olive oil into the meat and sprinkle some spices onto it. Cook it without covering for the first part if you want to brown all the surface. This is called broiling. Then wrap it in foil to retain the moisture and cook it. Any drippings and scraps of dried juices can be used for making gravy.

Poultry

Poultry should be roasted in the same way as other meat. You can also cook chicken in roasting bags. The advantage here is that you can sprinkle the seasoning inside, then shake the bag to cover the meat. Follow the guidelines that came with the bag to cook the chicken perfectly.

Chicken breast is quite tender and it can be cooked in just a few minutes in a frying pan, similar to cooking steaks.

Fish

Fish meat is quite tender and does not take long to cook. It is important not to overcook the fish. The fish is done when its colour changes from translucent to white. You can cook fish in the oven in 10 to 15 minutes at about 200°C to 230°C; pan fry it like steak for four to five minutes each side (here you can actually see the sides of the steak changing colour); or cook in a microwave in three to four minutes turning over half way through cooking. Fish is most suited for experimental cooks. Ideal fish to use are salmon or cod which is usually available without bones and comes in about one-inch thick pieces.

Eggs

Eggs are quite interesting as they contain two different types of proteins. The egg white, which is basically the food for the growing embryo contains 90% water and 10% protein. In its natural state this protein is loosely tangled up. Upon application of heat these strands stick to each other to form a firmer opaque mass. The egg yolk on the other hand contains 50% water, 30% fat and 20% protein. Due to its fat content it behaves differently on heating. The heat causes the yolk to form a thick crumbly mass.

Whisking the eggs causes air bubbles to form which pulls the proteins onto their surface. This forms a mass with air bubbles trapped inside which helps to create lightness in cakes, soufflés etc. Over-whisking should be avoided as it collapses the bubbles. For the same reason when whisked egg white is added to cake mixture it should be mixed gently so as not to disturb the bubble structure too much.

Eggs can be boiled, made into omelettes and cooked in a variety of ways such egg curry, scotch egg etc. and are ideal for experimental cooks.

Making stock, sauce, gravy

Making stocks, sauces and gravy involve similar processes. The recipes for making all these are easily available and simple to follow. In this section we are mainly concerned with how the chemistry of food affects the cooking of these items and to understand why the sauces, gravies etc. do not turn out as you expect.

Stock is made from meat or vegetables, often from left over uncooked vegetables or bones from uncooked meats that are unsuitable for other dishes. Stock is very useful for making soups and gravy. Stock can also be simply made from stock cubes, granules, or stockpots.

Cooked sauces are made from flour and milk, cream, or

grated cheese. They are used to flavour savoury as well as sweet dishes. There also cold sauces which are simply mixtures of various ingredients, for example tartare sauce. We are only concerned with cooked sauces here.

Gravy is usually made from the juices of baked, roasted or pan-fried meats and fortified with stock or wine (usually red wine). Gravy granules are also available. You can also fortify gravy with ingredients such as Marmite or Bovril or similar products. Gravy is used as a dressing for all kinds of baked or fried meat dishes, mashed potato, etc. It is often cooked with slightly caramelised sliced onions which gives a sweeter taste and a gelatine-like thick texture.

Role of starches in cooking of stock, sauces and gravy
Starches with a high associated protein content absorb more water and swell more than those with low protein content. When, during the process of cooking (while heating), the starch is added to water or any liquid, the starch molecules become sticky and tend to stick together which gives thickness to the gravy, sauce or stock.

The majority of the starches used in cooking are from either grains (for example flours), roots (for example arrowroot) or tubers (like potato flour); all with different properties, textures and flavours. We shall have a brief look at these properties.

Wheat flour and corn-starch are the most common forms of grain starches we use in our cooking. Because it is almost pure starch, corn-starch is a more efficient thickener than wheat flour. Both are medium-sized starch granules that gelatinise at a higher temperature than root starches. However, once the temperature is reached, thickening happens very quickly. Grain starches also contain a relatively high percentage of proteins, which makes sauces opaque and thick.

Root and tuber starches such as arrowroot or potato flour have a larger structure and require a comparatively lower temperature to cook. They produce a more translucent sauce, stock or gravy.

Choosing the starch for making sauce or gravy depends on a few factors. One consideration is whether you want to cook your sauce before you want to thicken it, for example a cheese sauce for pasta, or to add to meat stews. In that case use a grain starch. If you want to thicken the sauce before it is completely cooked then choose a root starch.

What happens to starches during the cooking process? How to avoid lumpy gravy?

If you mix flour into cold water, the starch granules absorb only a small amount of water and the granules will form clumps and sink to the bottom. If such a mixture is further heated the water will not further penetrate into them. This will result in a lumpy gravy. You need to add the flour to hot water or liquid like milk and continue heating and stirring. The molecules will stick together, the protein molecules denature and form a sticky network within the liquid, thus making it thick. For quick thickening without lumps use cornflour. **Cornflour is almost pure starch and a good**

thickening agent, although the taste using plain flour is different from that of corn flour.

For thickening curry sauces you can add flour the same way as for gravy. Chickpea flour (also called gram flour) is also used for this purpose. However, coconut milk and coconut cream are more popular as they impart a rich, flavoursome creamy taste to the dish.

This is an excellent area for the experimental cook to investigate and learn from. You will learn a lot from trying different starches and using different techniques.

Cooking vegetables

Most vegetables contain a larger amount of carbohydrates than proteins. They also contain fibre, vitamins and minerals. Always wash the vegetables thoroughly. Soak them in cold water for some time if they look a bit stale or tired: they will soon revive. Do not overcook the vegetables. In fact many vegetables can be eaten raw.

Vegetables can be stir-fried, steamed, used in curries, stews, pickled, used in salads, eaten raw with dips, and cooked as side dishes. It is best not to cook a leafy vegetable with the lid on as it changes colour and produces liquid which you do not want. Be careful with salt; most vegetables do not need much salt.

Some vegetables, like okra, contain protein that becomes sticky when heat is applied. This results in a sticky mass. You can get round this by adding acidity. Add tamarind paste

288

or sauce if you have some, or lemon juice or vinegar. This denatures the protein and when you stir the vegetables, the denatured protein is chopped into small pieces, thus taking away the sticky mess.

Cooking daals and pulses

Lentils are rich in proteins, fibre and minerals. The amount of protein differs depending upon the variety but on an average the lentils contain between 20 and 30% proteins. Red lentils are the best choice for the experimental cook, as well as the yellow moong daal. They have lots of flavour and are very easy to cook.

Always wash the lentils and soak them for at least an hour before cooking. Soaking moistens the cell walls which stretch, resulting in a softening of the interior. Use warm water if it is too cold. Cooking is easy, you will find some ideas of cooking daals in Part III of this book. Remember not to add the salt until the daal is nearly cooked because the salt slows down the absorption of water into the lentils.

ILLUSTRATIONS

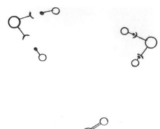

Figure 25A: A SIMPLIFIED EXPLANATION OF BONDING OF ATOMS

Top: Atoms with 'sockets' and 'balls'

Middle: connected as molecule

Bottom Chemical representation of H_2O (water)

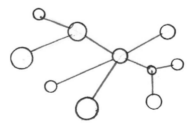

Figure 25B: Three dimensional structure of a molecule

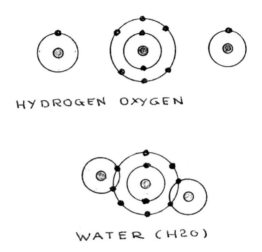

HYDROGEN OXYGEN

WATER (H₂O)

Figure 25C: ELECTRON SHARING

The above diagram shows atoms of hydrogen and oxygen with electrons orbiting around the central proton.

Top: Oxygen atom has six electrons in the outer orbit and space for two more electrons. The hydrogen atom has space for one more electron.

Bottom: Two hydrogen atoms combine with one oxygen atom sharing their electrons to from a water molecule.

Figure 25D: BEHAVIOUR OF PROTEIN MOLECULE

Above Left: In its natural state

Above Right: Denatured: long strings

Bottom: Chopped into smaller pieces during a process.

Figure 25E: STARCH MOLECULE

Left: Natural state. Right: After absorbing water.

Figure 25F: Starch molecules forming a network by sticking together after absorbing some water.

Figure 25G: Wet starch molecule network stretched as a result of kneading (such as in bread making)

26

WHAT CAN I DO WITH THESE?

SOME IDEAS FOR YOUR EXPERIMENTS

Here is a list of the most common ingredients and suggested uses for you to experiment with. The list is not exhaustive and does not include some of the most common uses; this would have been a boring and encyclopaedic exercise. I have listed some of the techniques that I have experimented with and found useful, and you can find more ideas on the internet. The idea here is to encourage you to experiment using similar techniques with other ingredients.

Breads, naans, parathas and wraps

ITEM	SUGGESTIONS
Bread slices	Toasted sandwiches (savoury and sweet) using banana and peanut butter, chutneys etc.
	Savoury and sweet egg fried bread, garlic bread: lightly toast then liberally spread garlic paste and warm the slice again under grill, enjoy with soups.
Soft Rolls	Make burgers with cheese, meats, and vegetables with sandwich toaster.
Stale bread	Make croutons, bread crumbs, make savoury croutons lightly fried in garlic butter, bread and butter pudding.

	Savoury dish: Crush by hand into tiny pieces (not crumbs), season with hot oil, garlic, green chilli and crushed peanuts, pinch of salt, cook three to four minutes with a couple of tablespoons of water, lid on: delicious!
Naans, parathas and chapattis Left over or dry	Sweet dish: cook the crushed pieces using golden syrup. Add vanilla essence if you wish.

Cereals and pulses

ITEM	SUGGESTIONS
Beans: moong and others	Sprouted beans: add to salads, soups and sandwiches
Porridge oats	Use for coating savoury cakes or meat/vegetable balls before frying (instead of semolina). Add to fruit crumble mixture for crunchy taste, use in home-made soups, make flapjacks
Pearl barley	Add to home-made soups.

Coleslaws, mayonnaise and sandwich spreads

ITEM	SUGGESTIONS
Mayonnaise	Make dressings similar to thousand island using chilli sauce, tomato ketchup and other sauces. Spread on bread instead of butter for sandwiches.

296

Coleslaw	Use as a salad ingredient with lettuce, tomato etc., add to jacket potatoes.
Sandwich spreads	Can also add to salads, to jacket potatoes, to prawn cocktail.

Foods cooked at home or bought from shops

ITEM	SUGGESTIONS
Leftover cooked meats	Add to soups, or add to stir-fry. Cut lamb/chicken pieces into small cubes and slowly shallow fry with very little oil: makes tasty snacks.
	Make patties.
	Make biryani: (also see morphing): add to cooked rice to make a biryani-type dish (moisten the pieces with a little yogurt, add a little red chilli powder and any masala if you wish, cook gently with the lid on for two or three minutes to heat it properly, mix with cooked rice in a microwaveable bowl, sprinkle/spray a little water, cover and microwave for about four or five minutes. Can add some chopped mint or mint jelly for extra flavour.
Left over vegetables	Check that they are in good condition to eat. Make veggie-burgers.

	Reheat with some butter and use again.
Potato mash	Use as topping for shepherd's pie, make potato rosti with chopped onion, green chilli, chopped coriander or mint and some lemon juice, rolled in semolina and lightly fried; potato meat balls with any leftover cooked meat.

Fruits, fresh and canned

ITEM	SUGGESTIONS
Apple (eating type)	Apple crumble, stewed apple stuffed with sultanas
Sharp tasting apples like Granny Smith or Bramleys	Green apple make excellent chutney (cut into small pieces, blitz with green chilli, chopped coriander, some garlic cloves, salt, lemon juice and pinch of sugar). Green apple pickle: use mango pickle mix (available from Asian shops) and follow the instructions on packet using green apples instead of raw mangoes. Lasts a long time. Add to vegetables to give an 'acidic bite'.
Avocado	Make avocado salad (with black pepper, salt, lemon juice), use in prawn cocktails. Make hummus (cooked chick peas, garlic cloves, lemon juice, tahini paste, blitz, add mayonnaise, black pepper, pinch of salt and small avocado pieces, stir to paste).

Banana	Tasty sweet dish with milk and ice cream, use with yogurt, make sandwiches with peanut butter on white or brown bread, toasted or untoasted.
	Halawa: crush banana, add desiccated coconut, some milk powder (optional), sultanas, brown sugar cook for a few minutes in ghee (or butter), spread in a pie dish and let it cool.
	Savoury sweet/sour vegetable: this works well both with ripe or slightly unripe banana (the taste will be different. Slice into thick circular slices, add chopped green chilli, some chopped coriander and some crushed peanuts to hot ghee or butter, toss in banana slices, cook for two or three minutes (lid off), add lemon juice and a pinch of salt, garnish with more chopped coriander (you can try garnishing with mint or any other herbs).
Canned fruit	Fruit salad, fruit trifle.
Orange/satsuma	In salads, fruit salads.
Canned pineapple slices	Great to oven bake ham and gammon with.

Meats and seafoods fresh and frozen

ITEM	SUGGESTIONS
All meats	Stews, curry, soups, grilled, barbecue, stir-fry, cold meats with salads, in sandwiches.

Cooked prawns	Cocktails, add to soups, stir-fry, add to rice, make prawn biryani, add to vegetables especially spinach, make curry with potato and/or mushrooms.
Sausages	Make curry, use in stir-fry. Use in sandwiches. Use the sausage meat to make meat balls or cakes.
Bacon	Bacon butty sandwich with fried bread, savoury bacon rice with green chilli and coriander.

Milk and yogurt

ITEM	SUGGESTIONS
Yogurt	Freeze yogurt in smaller containers, then when required use it for making lassi, sweet and sour banana dessert, and fruit yogurt using canned fruits. Refer to freezing tips in Section 6.
Milk	You can freeze milk (refer to freezing tips in Section 6). Excess milk can be used for making dessert dishes, milk shakes with ice-cream, creamy sauce, add a little to curries or stews in place of water, add to desiccated coconut to make it like fresh coconut (need to let it soak overnight and drain the excess milk), why not drink it as a night-cap?

Nuts

ITEM	SUGGESTIONS
Peanuts, cashew nuts	Add to chutneys, raitas, and salads.
	Savoury crispy peanuts and cashew nuts: refer to the recipe in Section 22, under snacks.
All nuts	Add where you need to provide crunchiness or texture, for example to cakes, pastry dishes, savoury drinks like lassi.

Vegetables, fresh, frozen and canned

ITEM	SUGGESTIONS
Aubergine	Make fritters (make round slices, cover with masala paste made from plain or gram flour with chilli and spices, shallow fry).
	Italian rice: add thin strips lightly cooked to cooked rice.
	Great as a vegetable either dry or with sauce cooked with tomato and potato: see Sections 10 and 20.
Beans	Add to stir-fry, to soups.
Beetroot	Make salad, raita (see Section 22).
Broccoli	Add to stir-fry, steam, add to home-made soup.
Canned beans	Add to soups, stews and curries, make savoury vegetable.

Cauliflower	Use to make raita (mix small florets or grated florets to tomato raita made with yogurt, sliced onion and green chilli), stir-fry florets in spices, make curry with potato, make spicy rice.
Celery	Add to meat dishes, use in home-made soups, salads, stir-fry.
Coriander	Use for garnishing, make chutney.
Corn on the cob	Add to meat and vegetable curries, roast or grill and rub over with a mixture of butter, black pepper and some salt.
Courgettes	Italian salad: using a potato peeler, peel into thin wide strips, put in a bowl, add olive oil, plenty of black pepper, lemon juice and salt, marinate for 20 to 30 minutes. Make simple vegetable: cut into small cubes (skin intact), season in hot oil with garlic and ginger slices and black pepper and pinch of salt. Can also cook with tomato as spicy vegetable.
Cucumber	Great for all types of raitas.
Leeks	Use in home-made soups, spicy vegetable.
Mushrooms	Add fresh mushrooms to ready-made cup-a-soups, add to curries and all meat dishes, stir-fry mushrooms in butter with cream sauce.
Okra	Savoury vegetable, add to meat curries, stuffed okra.

Onions	Make sauce for meat and vegetable dishes, add to salads, on its own with chopped chilli/black pepper, salt and lemon/vinegar, with meals/snacks, sprinkle finely chopped onion on savoury snacks. Add finely chopped onion to lassi drink. Microwave whole red onion with skin on, then peel. Lovely and sweet to eat, lovely flavour.
Peppers (all colours)	Make vegetable with potatoes, stuffed peppers with cooked prawns, use the baked casing for prawn cocktail, chopped peppers in salads, sliced peppers with hummus with drinks.
Potato	Make chips, spicy wedges, grated spiced (see Section 10), cook as dry vegetable (with or without onion) and fill it inside wraps or pancakes. Jacket potato, mash etc.
Spinach	Cook as vegetable, steam/microwave and add to soups.
Spring onions	Use in stir-fry, in salads.
Sweet potato	Grated and spiced same as potato, baked, chips/wedges, soup, add to other vegetables.
Tomato	Use in salads, sandwiches, raitas, soups, add to vegetable and meat dishes, green tomato chutney and vegetable dish.

27

WHERE TO GO FROM HERE

If you have followed this book and have experimented with your ideas, have tried out other people's recipes and have enjoyed the experience then here is something you could do to continue your experimenting, inventing new recipes and learning more.

1. List your ideas for lunch and dinners. That way you can plan your cooking time to suit your work or leisure time, and also plan your shopping.

2. Make a list of what you have in your fridge or freezer, add any more items you need to stock to your shopping list.

3. Make your own 'what can I do with these' list by category. For example meats, vegetables, sauces, dairy products etc. Add any of the items you have listed from the fridge or freezer list to this list. Now write down any ideas of how you can use them in the last column [what to do column].

4. Later on, see if you want to add any ideas from the above list to your ideas for lunches or dinners or snacks etc. This way you have a creative cycle of thinking, and experimenting.

5. Watch any cookery programmes you like to watch. You do not necessarily have to copy the recipe but you can get a lot of creative ideas on the techniques and use of various ingredients for experimenting with your own

recipes.

6. Cookery books are also a very good source for getting new ideas for your experimenting.

7. And finally if you feel confident then why not follow interesting recipes for a lunch or dinner from starter to dessert and enjoy with your invited guests?

Coming back to my analogy of painting:

I have practised and experimented with the art of watercolour. Now I have a collection of paintings that I show to my family and friends and they appreciate and enjoy looking at them.

You can do the same. Practise, experiment, look at the various recipes and you will be cooking dishes for your family and friends which I am sure they will enjoy.

28

FURTHER READING

There are a great number of cookery books from different cuisines. If you are interested in the science of cooking I can recommend the following, which I found useful.

The Science of Cooking by Peter Barham. London: Springer, 1950.

Culinary Reactions: The Everyday Chemistry of Cooking by Simon Quellen Field. Chicago: Chicago Review Press, 2012.

Keys to Good Cooking: A Guide to Making the Best of Foods and Recipes by Harold McGee. London: Hodder and Stoughton, 2010.

Organic Chemistry: A Brief Survey of Concepts and Applications by Philip Bailey and Christina Bailey. Boston, MA: Allyn & Bacon, 1978.

ILLUSTRATIONS:

Following sources are gratefully acknowledged:

Electron sharing: Figure 25 C adapted from:
Hidden In Plain Sight 5: Atom by Andrew Thomas, Aggrieved Chipmunk Publications 2016

Protein and Starch molecules: Figures 25 D, 25 E, 25 F and 25 G adapted from:
The Science of Cooking by Peter Barham. London: Springer, 1950.

Index

Basic information

About the book and walk through 7
Basic kit for starters 65
Cleaning pots and pans: burnt .. .. .120
Disaster recovery 81-82
Distractions: dealing with 19-20
Kitchen management.. 17-20
Knife 26
List of spices 100-107
Onion chopping techniques. 45-46
Part processes 19
Planning... 18
Processes and techniques. 43-58
Science of cooking 15-58
Steamer 29
Storing Coriander 22
Storing foods and ingredients 21-24, 116, 130
Storing Potatoes 21
Storing yogurt 22
Timers. 20
Vegetables 163-165
Wok 25-26, 50, 56

Breads

Baking bread. 51-52
Bread... 149-150
Freezing bread ... ... .119
Parathas ... ... .149

Chemistry of cooking

Basic information

Atoms.. 271-272
Bond ... ... .272
Carbohydrates... 274-276
Denaturing of proteins 37
Enzymes 41, 54, 276
Fibres .. .. .276
Gelatine ... ... .273
Molecule.. ... ... .271
Oils saturated, unsaturated, hydrogenated ... ... .277
Pectin .. .. .276
Proteins ... ... .273
Proteins water loving and hating ... ... .274
Starches 38, 274-276
Sugars 39

Chemistry of cooking processes

Baking. 51
Choosing starch for sauce 285-288
Cooking leg of lamb ... ... .283
Cooking steaks .. .. .283
Cooking tough and tender meats... 281-282
Cooking vegetables, pulses and daals.. 288-289
Deep frying... ... ... .279
Grilling 49, 140, 278
Lumpy gravy. ... ... .287
Making stock, sauce and gravy.. ... ...116, 285
Maillard reaction ... ... .115
Roasting... ... ...139, 280
Role of starches in making sauces and gravies... ... ... .286
Steaming.. 48

Cooking foods: general (refer to part III)

Breads 51, 149-150
Chicken 75, 115, 151, 241
Cooking with spices: rough guide to proportions 124-128

Desserts 257-266
Fish 151-152, 284
Making gravy 116, 274, 285-287
Making sauces ... ... .285
Meats .. .. .115
Mushrooms.. ... ... .114
Pasta 143-145, 253
Potatoes 139-141
Rice 129-138
Soups 69, 159-161
Sprouted pulses. ... ... .158
Steak ... ... 115, 151, 278 ,283
Vegetables 113-114, 163-165

Processes and techniques

Baking 51-52, 280
Blanching. 54
Boiling and steaming.. 48
Braising 49
Bread making 51-52
Chopping, cutting and slicing food 44-45
Cooking in a bag 55-56
Cooking in a foil 55-56
Cooking with a wok 56
Freezing... 53-54
Freezing chutney ... ... .118
Freezing milk ... ... .119
Freezing yogurt 53, 119
Frying deep... 50
Frying shallow... 50
Grated coconut substitute for fresh ... ... .121
Grilling 49-50
Hot oil seasoning 57
Marinades 46-47
Moroccan tagine 57
Morphing 85-86
Onion chopping 45-46

Onion cooking.. 107-109
Parboiling 49
Poaching.. 55
Saffron how to use. 236, 258
Simmering 49
Slow cooking 52
Smoking food 110-111, 232
Smoking Biryani 232, 237
Sprouting using sprouting jar 157-158
Steamed vegetables 29-30
Stir frying. 50
Vinaigrettes using... 48

Recipe and ideas for beginners

Avocado salad 68
Baked fish 74
Baked potato variations 72
Banana dessert... 79
Cheese on toast. 72
Chicken in roasting bag... 75
Chilli oil 68
Chow Mein.. 77
Fruit salad 80
Fruit trifle 80
Fruit yogurt 79
Gammon and pine apple 76
Garlic toast 70
Potato wedges 141
Prawn/ ham cocktail 66
Raitas 69
Rice noodle variations. 77-78
Salads 67-68
Sausage stir fry... 74
Sausages and baked beans and onion gravy.. 74
Soups 69-70
Spicy couscous 76
Spicy spinach 78